# Earth Healing

This is an IndieMosh book

brought to you by MoshPit Publishing
an imprint of Mosher's Business Support Pty Ltd

PO Box 147
Hazelbrook NSW 2779

indiemosh.com.au

Copyright © Dr Mahdi Mason 2017

The moral right of the author has been asserted in accordance with the Copyright Amendment (Moral Rights) Act 2000.

All rights reserved. Except as permitted under the Australian Copyright Act 1968 (for example, fair dealing for the purposes of study, research, criticism or review) no part of this publication may be reproduced, stored in a retrieval system, or transmitted in any form or by any means, electronic, mechanical, photocopying, recording or otherwise, without the written permission of the publisher.

Cataloguing-in-Publication entry is available from the National Library of Australia: http://catalogue.nla.gov.au/

| | |
|---|---|
| Title: | Earth Healing: Healing the Earth to Heal Ourselves |
| Author: | Mason, Mahdi |
| Illustrator: | Kathy Gardiner |
| ISBNs: | 978-1-925666-85-4 (paperback) |
| | 978-1-925666-62-5 (ebook – epub) |
| | 978-1-925666-63-2 (ebook – mobi) |

The author has made every effort to ensure that the information in this book was correct at the time of publication. However, the author and publisher accept no liability for any loss, damage or disruption incurred by the reader or any other person arising from any action taken or not taken based on the content of this book. The author recommends seeking third party advice and considering all options prior to making to decisions or taking action in regard to the content of this book.

Cover design by Mahdi Mason and Ally Mosher

Cover layout by Ally Mosher at allymosher.com

Cover images from Shutterstock.com

Theme illustrations by Kathy Gardiner

# *Earth Healing*

## Healing the Earth to Heal Ourselves

### DR MAHDI MASON

## *Also by Dr Mahdi Mason*

The Power of You: How to Positively Influence People, Places and the World

# *Acknowledgements*

To all the beautiful animals on this planet, thank you for uplifting me on a daily basis. Thank you for opening my heart and for teaching me how to approach life. You are my passion and the reason I've followed my life path. From the bottom of my heart, I wish you love, safety and respect from all human beings.

My wonderful friends and family, every day I am grateful to have such an amazing bunch of people in my life. Without your love and support, I'm sure I never would have had the guts to follow each one of my dreams—this book being one. Thank you for making me laugh, cry and feel loved regularly.

To my guides in spirit, thank you for walking me through this journey and helping me to feel inspired. My stubborn human ways have no doubt made you want to scream in frustration on more than one occasion, but you have always stuck with me. Mother Earth, thank you for choosing me to share your message. I hope this book does you some justice.

Sara Jones, thank you for being my go-to gal whenever I've needed support on this Earth healing journey. You've always known exactly where I was coming from and the right things to say. I hope we do some serious Earth healing together while we're here.

Kathy Gardiner, my illustrator and amazing friend, thank

you for the magnificent job you have done and for bringing your magical energy into this book. I feel so proud every time I look at the front cover.

Lauren Marks, my editor, thank you for spending so much time making sense of my words and for taking my work to the next level. Your level of professionalism has instilled more confidence in me for the work I release to the world.

Kristal Brown, you angel, the rest of my Thursday girls and my Soulpreneur friends, thank you for your belief in my work and ongoing encouragement.

Amanda Dillon, thank you for reading through my manuscript, and making sense of it. I can't wait for the world to hear your message also.

Maggie Landman, thank you so much for teaching me the art of energetic Earth healing. I knew I was an Earth Healer long before I knew how to actually do it, and you came into my life right when I needed you. You were the perfect teacher, encouraging me when I needed it and stepping out of the way to let me learn on my own when it was time for me to step up. You have done so much for the planet and I am honoured to know you.

Carren Smith, not only my speaking coach but also my mentor, thank you for running with the message of this book from the second you heard about it. Your support for my work has done wonders for my confidence and future dreams. Bless you for being such an Earth angel.

To the incredible Earth Healers and conservationists who have come before me—the likes of Dr Jane Goodall, Sir David Attenborough, Steve Erwin, Lyn White and Anna

Breytenbach—thank you for leading the way. Thank you for never giving up. Thank you for showing the world how incredible nature really is.

# Dedication

*I dedicate this book to Mother Earth and all of her wondrous creatures.*

# Contents

Introduction ........................................................................... 1
   My story ............................................................................. 3

**Chapter 1: What is 'Earth healing'?** ................................. 9
   It's all energy .................................................................... 15
   How we interfere with the flow of energy ............................ 17
   The process of becoming a powerful Earth Healer................ 24

**Chapter 2: The modern Earth Healer** ........................... 25

**Chapter 3: Mother Earth gives you everything you need to survive** ................................................................................. 33
   Food ................................................................................. 38
   Water ................................................................................ 39
   Air ..................................................................................... 40
   Shelter ............................................................................... 41
   Medicine ........................................................................... 42
   Recreation ......................................................................... 43
   Upliftment ......................................................................... 43
   Wisdom ............................................................................ 46

**Chapter 4: Connecting to the Earth** .............................. 49
   What does connecting to the Earth actually mean?............. 51
   How did we get so disconnected? ....................................... 53
   Why it's important to connect with nature .......................... 54
   How to reconnect with nature ............................................ 58

**Chapter 5: Embracing the feminine** ............................... 67
   10 benefits of embracing your feminine energy ................... 72
   10 ways to embody your sacred feminine ............................ 75

## Chapter 6: Lessening your environmental impact ........... 81
Find your 'Why?' ............................................................................ 84
Reducing your physical environmental footprint ....................... 85
It's more than just a physical thing ............................................. 95
Reducing your metaphysical environmental footprint ............... 98

## Chapter 7: Physically healing the Earth ....................... 107
Recreating healthy ecosystems ................................................ 110
Let it burn ................................................................................. 112
15 ways to physically give back to the Earth ........................... 113

## Chapter 8: Metaphysically healing the Earth ................ 123
Healing with love, gratitude and intention .............................. 127
5 ways to increase your intention ............................................ 129
5 ways to energetically give back to the Earth ........................ 130

## Chapter 9: The end game .............................................. 137
10 ways you can manifest healing for Mother Earth ............... 140

## Chapter 10: She will thank you ..................................... 147
Mother Nature and her gifting ways ....................................... 149

## Chapter 11: We are all Mother Earth's children ............. 159
He's not heavy, he's my brother .............................................. 161
Working together for positive outcomes ................................ 164

## Chapter 12: Ascension of the planet ............................ 175
What you can do to help the Earth ascend ............................. 180

## Author's final word ...................................................... 187

## About the Author ........................................................ 191

# Introduction

Do you feel anxious about the current state of the globe? Feel like we are all doomed here on planet Earth? I don't blame you if you do. On a daily basis, most of the media only focuses on the destruction and negative things humankind are doing to the Earth.

They show us gut-wrenching pictures of entire forests being decimated by logging, polar bears starving due to climate change and entire cities blanketed in man-made smog. They show us whales caught in shark nets, major oil spills and rare animals being hunted by poachers. They show us these images and then leave us there to try and make sense of it all.

The media leave us in a state of fear and hate—fear that the world will end tomorrow; fear that there's nothing we can do about it. Hate for all the people causing the disturbance. They offer no solutions and no way forward.

We have a choice in how we react to these reports. We can sit back in fear and do nothing, we can waste our energy pointing fingers at everyone else and say how dreadful they are, or we can use that energy and be the change we want to see in the world. As in any situation in need of a solution, there are ways to be constructive and ways to be destructive. Only focusing on what is wrong, without proposing a way forward, is destructive.

As environmentalists, eco-warriors, healers and

lightworkers, we already know the state of the planet. We don't need to see it in the media. We feel the pain of Mother Earth and all of her living creatures. We know it's time to take action in order to sustain human life for many generations to come.

What many of us don't know is what we can do to make a difference. You are just one person in a world of billions, and the extent of destruction is so massive that it's nearly impossible to believe you could have any effect. I am here to tell you that *there are things you can do that will make a difference*. This book will show you how.

There's also a great shift in consciousness taking place around the world, an 'ascension'. As part of this process, people are becoming more aware of their impacts on the environment. More so, we want to be kinder to the planet and heal the Earth, but where to start?

There are many well-known ways of reducing our environmental footprint and if you are reading this book, chances are you already do many of those things. You probably limit your water usage, avoid single-use items where possible and recycle or upcycle. You might ride your bike to work or catch public transport to lessen the number of cars on the road. All of these things are great and they are necessary steps towards improving the way we treat the environment (there's even a chapter on how to reduce your impact in this book). But reducing our impact doesn't stop our destruction of the Earth. It doesn't reverse it. It only slows it down. Even when we reduce our impact, we are still increasing our environmental footprint.

Given the state of the environment across the globe, we can no longer be satisfied with simply reducing our impact. We need to take things a step further. We need to start *reversing* the damage we have done and start supporting the natural systems and cycles in nature that we are very much a part of.

Becoming an Earth Healer is the best way to help the planet become healthier, happier and able to sustain an abundance of life once again. It is something every single person can do and it can be done within every person's means. Best of all, no matter where you live in the world, or what your situation, you can start today. Earth healing is incredibly easy. You don't have to have studied courses, spent years in an ashram or lived in the Amazon Jungle learning how to live in harmony with nature. Once you realise all the things you can do *right now* to help heal the Earth, you'll want to begin straight away.

If we, as global citizens, want to make Mother Earth healthy again (and yes, it is possible), we can no longer depend on conservationists and green groups to do it for us. It needs to be a concerted effort by the wider population. It is a mammoth task, the work that needs to be done to heal the Earth, and a mammoth task requires many hands including yours.

## My story

My passion for helping animals and the environment has

been life long. As I sit here in my home office with one of my dogs curled up at my feet, staring at the poorly put-together vision board of what I hope this book will achieve (I was never great at arts and craft), I realise that I believe in the power of humanity and the possibility that we can all live in harmony with nature.

My fascination with nature started when I was a small child, perhaps even from birth. It all started with a love of animals, really. It didn't matter which species, I was besotted and thought them all to be my friends.

Well before I started school, I can remember not being able to watch the suffering of fish that had just been caught, or bugs drowning in the pool. I would always save them wherever I could. I can distinctly remember yelling at boys who were throwing rocks at birds, telling them what I thought of them, without a care in the world about what they thought of me.

I was always passionate and fearless when it came to the wellbeing of animals. To me, they were all innocent creatures just trying to survive in this world. Who were we to decide their fate? We have no more right to be here than they do. We just have the mental capacity and physical ability to dominate them. As a society, we abuse that power daily.

In primary school, I started to learn that no one animal is separate from the environment in which it lives. What each animal does has an impact on the vegetation, the soil, the creek, the food chain and other animals. It is part of a larger system. So to protect animals, I had to learn about different environments, climates, ecosystems, their physical makeup, etc.

In my final years of high school, my elective subjects consisted of biology, chemistry, maths, geography and the study of society. All formed the foundation of knowledge that I would need to go on to study environmental science at university.

Throughout university, I also took the opportunity to volunteer on wildlife conservation projects to get an understanding of the issues facing particular species. One such project, which I have very fond memories of, was a rehabilitation centre for gibbons in Thailand. The dedication of the staff there was incredibly inspiring.

Just after I finished my bachelor's degree, I began taking courses in metaphysics, healing, yoga and anything to do with being a lightworker. I had been interested in spirituality since childhood, but had never undertaken any formal study. Those courses led me down the path of becoming an energetic healer and eventually a shamanic practitioner (which I still practice as today). I especially love shamanism because it combines all of my interests—animals, nature, healing and spirituality.

My undergraduate environmental degree set me in good stead to start a successful career in environmental management. My work enabled me to travel overseas three times a year on holidays, drive a sports car, complete a master's degree and a doctorate, and move into an executive position within my first six years of working.

I spent every holiday either traveling around the world to spend time with Indigenous peoples in their native cultures, seeing animals in their natural habitats, or hiking in the wilderness. I was fortunate enough to see oranguatans in Borneo, blue-footed boobies in the Galápagos Islands (my favourite place in the whole world!), and mountain gorillas in Uganda, to name a few.

I hiked some of the world's greatest hiking trails such as the Annapurna Circuit in Nepal, Mount Kilimanjaro, the El Camino de Santiago in Spain and the Lares Trek in Peru. Each one was so magical that it left me wanting to plan my next adventure somewhere else. I don't think that desire will ever leave me.

Much of my Earth healing wisdom came from spending time with first nations' peoples in various places around the globe. All of them had a similar relationship with Mother Earth—they respected her and never took anything for granted. They understood that they depended on her and that she looked after them, providing them with everything they needed for survival.

I worked in mining and there was no doubt in my mind that I was meant to be there. I saw myself as working on the front line. Being in a position to effectively create change and reduce the impact on the environment from the inside, rather than being an activist on the outside (who I knew companies wouldn't listen to).

But eventually, I fell off my high horse. I realised that my labours weren't really making a difference in the overall scheme of things. Despite my best efforts, I still dealt with people who had no respect, compassion or desire to help Mother Earth on a daily basis. I watched entire landscapes be bulldozed, dug up, depleted of resources and covered back over with little attempt to make the ecosystems healthy again.

I investigated incidents of workers pumping polluted water into creeks and purposely running over wildlife. I saw people dumping oil on the ground and down drains. And I watched as people discarded their waste wherever they liked because they couldn't be bothered finding a bin.

The worst thing about it all? No-one ever had gratitude for the things the Earth had given them—the resources that created jobs for them, fed their families and made them wealthy. No-one cared about how much time and energy Mother Earth had put into creating these resources. There was a complete imbalance between what was being taken and what was being given back.

I realised that until I did something to correct that imbalance, I wasn't effectively helping Mother Earth at all. All of my efforts were just BAND-AID solutions that never addressed the underlying problem. A radical shift in the way we managed the environment was needed. And that's what has led me to write this book.

The following chapters explain how we need to change our entire perception about the environment and our place in the natural systems of the planet. It then goes on to provide practical advice on how, during our daily lives, we can start to make the natural world healthy again.

You'll see me refer to Mother Earth as 'Mother Nature' and simply 'Earth'. It is all the same thing to me no matter what you call it—Gaia, Pacha Mama or whatever other name you may use. It's the energy that supports all life and manages all elements on this planet.

No concept in this book is difficult to comprehend, nor is any suggested action difficult to undertake. Earth healing is simple and achievable by all. It is also the highest order of service on the planet right now.

# Chapter 1: What is 'Earth healing'?

The term 'Earth healing' may sound like some sort of 'out there' alternative practice, but the truth is, it is for all people. You don't have to have a background in environmental management, be into spirituality or believe in the benefits of alternative healing modalities. All you need is a desire to help the planet (and hopefully this book will give you all the reasons you need to want to do that).

Earth healing is the simple practice of giving back to the Earth. It can be as scientific or as mystical as you like. It can be a physical or metaphysical effort. The main thing is that energy is being sent back into the Earth after we have taken energy from it.

*Earth healing is the simple practice of giving back to the Earth.*

Modern, non-indigenous society has lost touch with the Earth. It has forgotten that we are part of numerous natural systems—ecosystems—and that when we take from Mother Nature, we are supposed to give something in return. Ecosystems are cycles. They don't work if one process stops feeding the next.

In any ecosystem, each component (whether it be a plant, insect, bird or other animal) is designed to take something it needs for survival, utilise it and pass on its waste, which will be utilised by another component of the system. Think of a tree, for example—to grow, it will *take* nutrients from the soil, sunlight from the sun, water from rain and carbon from the air. In return, it will *give* food, shelter, oxygen for animals and humans. And when it dies, it provides organic matter that will return to the soil as nutrients, making it fertile ground to support new plant life.

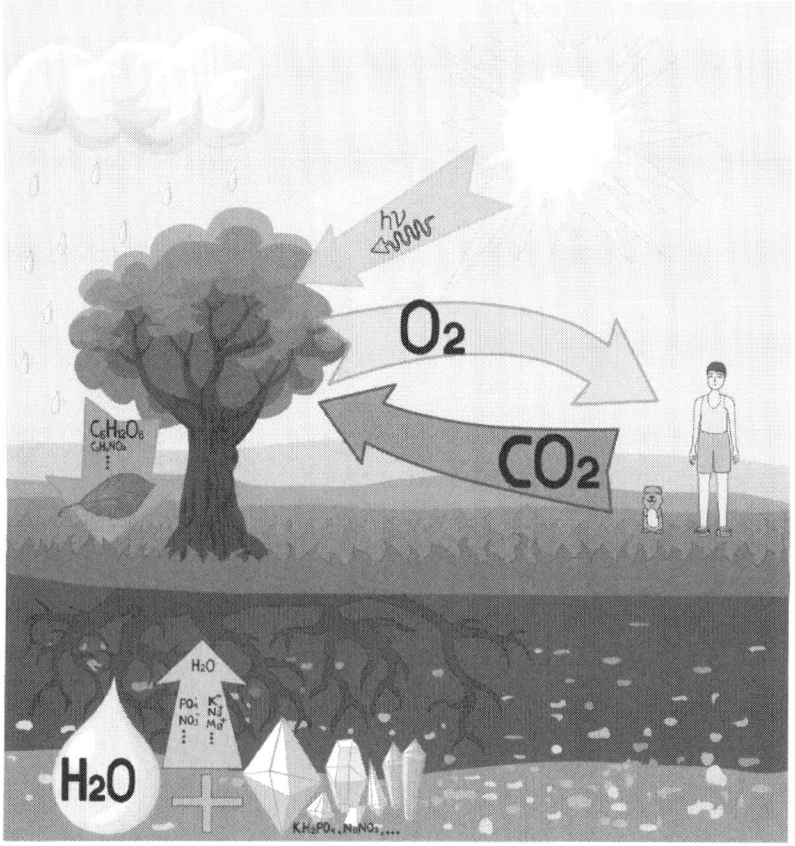

*Figure 1: A tree playing its part in its ecosystem*

As humans, we take anything and everything we like from ecosystems—often things that are not even necessary for our survival. We rarely give anything of use to nature in return.

We take trees, water, minerals, animals, fossil fuels and anything we can see a use for. What's worse is that we waste most of it.

If we ever do release something back into the environment, it's usually in the form of pollution—materials that are toxic to ecosystems and cause much harm to the biota. As if raping and pillaging the natural world isn't enough, we have to take things a step further and destroy it from the inside out.

There is a huge disparity in what we take from the Earth and what we give back (that's of use to the environment). It's making the ecosystems very unbalanced and unsustainable. In other words, the ecosystems are unable to support life.

When we do play our part in our surrounding ecosystems and support the other components within them, we are in harmony with nature. When we are in harmony with nature, we are healthy and so is it. It's only when we start going against the laws of nature that we cause problems for all involved.

Undisturbed ecosystems are actually quite resilient. Millions of years of evolution has enabled them to be in a constant state of equilibrium. Everything has a role, nothing dominates and nothing goes to waste. The systems are whole, self-sustaining and all together, one strong unit.

When we humans start disrupting ecosystems, we create holes in their natural armour. We make them unstable and weak. The systems are no longer able to defend or sustain themselves as well as they did before. That then leaves these ecosystems open to destruction from the elements, new species, viruses and the like.

As soon as one part of the ecosystem becomes weak, the rest of the system is impacted. Every disturbance has a much wider impact than the specific area disturbed, because every animal, plant or structure has a part to play in the system. So, every entity is impacted through an inability to function correctly and/or the disturbance itself.

If we don't start playing our part and giving back to nature, we will shut down the natural cycles and ecosystems. That means we shut ourselves down too. Not only will we wipe out the majority of species on the planet (who are just minding their own business and trying to survive, I might add), we will wipe out ourselves as well.

So, it doesn't really matter whether you are a nature lover or an egocentric megalomaniac who couldn't care less about the environment. Not giving back to the Earth will affect you the same. It will bring an end to you, your family and everything you have ever worked for. It's a harsh reality, but it's not too late to turn things around.

Consider Earth healing as recharging the planet. Mother Earth can only give to us what she is able to produce. If we only ever take from her, and never replenish her energy, she becomes unable to re-stock all the foods and materials we need to survive.

By not recharging the Earth, we are not replenishing our own food, water, shelter and resource reserves. Now, I'm not the world's greatest genius, but the fact that we aren't doing this sounds a little silly to me—we are slowly killing ourselves.

Another way of thinking of Earth healing is to pay, for what we take from the Earth, in the form of energy. Instead of seeing Mother Nature's products and services as free, like most of us currently do, we should see it as something we have to pay for. Just as we pay for every other good and service in our lives.

You pay for what you take, or give in return for what you receive. Paying for what we take from the Earth is a way of giving thanks. It's a way of acknowledging what is given to us to live our lives, but it also helps the Earth to sustain us living on it.

The Incas called this 'Ayni'. It was the philosophy or reciprocity—when you take something, you give something in return. It meant living in proper relationship with the environment, where one doesn't have a net negative impact on it.

## It's all energy

When I first started studying different schools of thought on spirituality, the one thing that was repeated over and over again was the concept of everything being energy. It's a major construct of yoga, reiki, Qi Gong, acupuncture, kinesiology, shamanism, Buddhism and most likely any eastern or Indigenous belief system. I found myself always explaining things to friends and family using the principal, almost to the point of rolling my eyes at myself for becoming one of those people who always talked about the same thing.

Food is energy, sunlight is energy, what our bodies are made up of is energy, trees are energy, wind is energy, cars are energy, tables are energy, thoughts are energy, sounds are energy, emotions are energy and spirit is energy. They are all just in different forms, vibrating at different states.

Everything on this planet is energy! The planet itself is energy!

The idea of everything being energy makes sense to me. In fact, I don't really understand why it is considered alternative to think that way. Having studied science at university, I know that scientists and academics are happy to state that the Universe is made up of atoms, molecules and matter and that they can be of solid, liquid or gaseous form. But suggest the concept of humans having a non-visible energetic body, or their consciousness being related to different vibrational states and they go running.

I guess the big disparity in views between science and spirituality is the metaphysical—that which what can't be seen (yet!), or is beyond the physical. However, my experience in energetic healing has taught me that both types of energy, physical and metaphysical, can be utilised for beneficial purposes; and both are very much real.

The physical/visible aspects of ecosystems and planetary cycles are well documented in science. You've probably seen those diagrams depicting how water is transformed through solid (ice), liquid (surface water and groundwater) and gas (evaporation/transpiration) and transported around the planet? Maybe you've seen similar diagrams for the carbon cycle and nutrient cycle?

What aren't so common are diagrams of the metaphysical energy cycles; the ones that show the different energies being passed on between people, animals, the Earth and the Universe. Although these energy flows through nature are well understood by ancient cultures (such as Hindu and Buddhist), they are not so well documented.

*Figure 2: An abstract illustration of the complexity of energy flows in nature.*

## How we interfere with the flow of energy

As humans, we need a range of different energies to survive. Physically, we need energy in the form of food, air and water. Energetically, we need energy in the form of life force energy, love and a range of other emotions, thoughts, confidence, sexual satisfaction, creativity and self-expression, wisdom, connection; the list goes on.

We receive and release both physical and metaphysical energy on a daily basis. When we are not mindful of where we are getting energy from, and where we are discharging it to, we can be destructive to the world around us. If we do not manage the energy in accordance with natural systems, we cause problems for ourselves and the systems as well.

Energy likes to flow. More than that, it has a universal predisposition of how it likes to flow. Given the chance to flow without interference, it will flow in balance with the rest of the system—in a constant state of equilibrium. That is how energy should flow through us on Earth. But it doesn't because we interfere with our own agendas.

Irrespective of which natural cycle it is on Earth, and whether you believe in the metaphysical systems or not, we humans must stop blocking the flow of energy by assuming it's all about us. We need to pass on some of the energy we receive to the rest of the natural world so that the environment can function as it was designed to—sustainably.

We need to be giving back to Mother Earth. We need to be Earth healing.

**Physical energy blocks**

With the development of cities, urbanisation and industrialisation comes the clearing of vegetation, land and natural ecosystems. Every time we change an undisturbed area through a new land-use, we take energy out of the natural system. We cause an energy block.

The system that would have otherwise been continually fed at the ground level with nutrients from organic matter (i.e. dropped tree leaves, branches, animal waste), rainwater, sunlight and more, now gets nothing. It most likely gets covered in impermeable concrete or bitumen, and any runoff water gets redirected to the ocean.

A very simple (yet not very pretty) example of we how commonly block the natural energy flow on a daily basis is the way we treat dog poo. We feed our dogs lots of food (energy) and when they excrete their waste, we pick it up in plastic bags and then place it into a bin. That's instead of allowing it to decompose into the soil and replenish the Earth with nutrients (energy).

I understand the hygienic reasons behind picking up dog poo. However, that doesn't mean that we should send it all to landfill. We could easily have drop off locations or bins where the contents could eventually be utilised by the Earth.

Another way we block the energy flow is by taking excessive resources from the Earth to make products for ourselves, but then send the majority of our waste to lined landfills. So much of our waste could be given back to the Earth to be transformed into nutrients and minerals. Instead, we send it to pits that are purposely segregated from the natural environment.

According to Annie Leonard (Executive Director of Greenpeace US and leader of the push to change the way we make, use and discard items), 99% of what we purchase goes to waste disposal facilities within the first six months. That's to landfill and recycling, not back into the soil to replenish it. Recycling is a good thing as it prevents the need for more materials to be taken from the Earth, but it still takes energy and resources out of the original system and blocks the flow of energy back into it.

What's worse is that it's estimated that 50% of what goes to landfill is food or green waste (according to my local council, Brisbane City Council). Food and green waste could easily be given back to the environment. Now, I'm not suggesting that we should dump all our waste in nature. Obviously, there are many harmful chemicals and bi-products that would harm not only the environment, but also us if we were to place that waste in uncontrolled locations. All I'm saying is that so much of what we send to landfill could actually benefit nature and give energy back to it.

The manipulation and diversion of water catchment areas to benefit people also blocks natural energy flows. Instead of water collecting naturally, picking up nutrients and spreading them over large areas, it is funnelled into fewer, often man-made, high-flow channels. This means the water picks up nutrients from landscapes before rushing through these channels and then dumps those nutrients into the ocean (where it causes problems for the oceanic ecosystems).

Another way that humans have damaged natural energy cycles of the planet, and which is proving to have catastrophic consequences, is damage caused to the carbon cycle. We pull carbon out of the ground in the form of fossil fuels and gasses and release it into the atmosphere when we consume those things for energy (petrol and electricity, for example). We also take away much of the naturally occurring energy sinks, such as trees, which would usually take in the atmospheric carbon and store it for us.

This leaves surplus carbon in the air—much more than can be stored by natural carbon sequesters. To make matters worse, the excess carbon is a greenhouse gas that helps the planet to hold heat in the atmosphere (i.e. global warming). As the planet heats up, more carbon is released into the atmosphere from the oceans, etcetera, which can no longer retain the carbon at that temperature. It's an ever-expanding problem.

A further case of poor energy management is primary production in Australia. Instead of looking at what our natural landscapes and climates could actually support, or copying what Indigenous peoples of the land did, we introduced agricultural methods from Europe. Europe! I don't think the two natural environments could be any more different!

So, to support European agricultural methods in Australia, we've had to clear huge areas of land for livestock (because pasture doesn't grow as densely here), transport water thousands of kilometres to water crops (because there aren't enough local water reserves), and severely damage primary production land due to the introduction of hooved animals (rather than local species that don't impact the land as much).

Then we've had to control all the feral animals that have run rampant because we've wiped out all of the naturally occurring ecosystems and made lands more suitable for introduced species. We've been fighting against Mother Nature to produce our food. Or to put it in Australian terms, 'We've been pushing shit uphill!'.

It really is ludicrous. All of this time we could have been living in harmony with the land. We would have saved so much energy. Instead, we've pretty much made things as hard as humanly possible for ourselves.

We've taken on Mother Nature in our food production fight and most people are slowly coming to the conclusion that we are losing. Our lands are no longer productive, cattle farming is significantly contributing to climate change and we don't have enough water supply to keep irrigating the thousands of acres of crops.

## Mind, body and spirit energy blocks

Human minds are very powerful. Most people don't realise the power they have to create happier lives for themselves and others. Sadly, we tend to use our brainpower to worry about things and try and control situations (of this, I have been guilty many a time). That, of course, only leads to misery.

Our minds are often the culprits when it comes to blocking the natural flow of energy. We shut down and prevent or restrict the flow of energy through our bodies by not allowing things to just be as they are, by not accepting situations in our lives and holding on to emotional wounds, through having limiting beliefs about ourselves and not standing in our power (to name but a few).

The term 'just go with the flow' exists for good reason! The more we resist it, the more problems it causes for us. As hard as it is, accepting whatever hardships come our way is the healthiest thing for our planet and us. Sometimes we just need to get out of our own way and let nature run its course.

Negative thoughts also restrict energy flow. They are lower in vibration and denser, which means the negative energy is harder to shift. You can support the Earth and its ascension (see Chapter 12) by choosing to have a positive mindset.

Energy flow around the body is also important in the overall scheme of planetary energy flows. We restrict how the energy flows through our bodies by eating foods that are synthetic, toxic and lacking nourishment, by being sedentary and through pushing ourselves too hard for too long. The greater the build-up of toxins, gunk and weight, the less energy can flow in and around your body.

We can also restrict the flow of spirit by clogging our energy centres, being stressed out, being unbalanced, being fearful and shutting ourselves off from certain experiences. The flow of spirit and life force energy is important for our wellbeing, and for the wellbeing of Mother Earth. If life force energy can't flow, life can't exist.

## The process of becoming a powerful Earth Healer

Earth healing is the act of giving back to the Earth—physically or metaphysically. However, there are certain things you can and should do prior to, as they will help you to be a more effective healer. They include:

- reducing your environmental impact
- developing a strong connection with Mother Earth
- embracing feminine energy
- seeing all people and living things as children of the Earth and therefore equal
- staying focussed on the world we want to create

  and

- supporting Mother Earth through the process of planetary ascension.

The following chapters go into each of these steps in more detail. They are all important in re-establishing the natural energy flows of the planet and they will assist you to become the most powerful Earth Healer you can be.

# Chapter 2: The modern Earth Healer

Historically, in Indigenous cultures, everyone was an Earth Healer. It wasn't a prestigious title that was only given to select few. Everyone appreciated what Mother Earth did for him or her and they didn't take anything she gave them for granted.

Indigenous peoples all over the world—our ancestors—lived in harmony with the land. When they took something, they gave something else back; be it was through gratitude, ceremony or physical gifts. They understood that they were part of a larger natural system and, that to continue to survive, they had to participate in keeping it going.

These people never took more than they needed and they only took what they could use. Any more than that was a burden and would require space and energy to manage; they would have to acquire this space and energy from nature, so they saw no point in being greedy.

Unlike our modern cultures, there was no respect or hierarchy for people who collected the most material things, so there was no competition to attain as much as they could. They didn't lose sight of where their materials came from, so they didn't rape and pillage the land in the name of becoming more powerful.

Our ancestors also never wasted what Mother Nature gifted to them. If they caught an animal, they would use the flesh for food; skin for clothing; teeth, claws and bones for jewellery and tools; and other remains for glue. Everything had a use.

They also always asked nature before taking anything and didn't assume they had rights to everything. Respect was given to each and every plant, stream, rock, creepy crawly and animal. Our ancestors understood that, just like them, much energy had gone into creating each of these and to disregard that was to disregard life itself.

In addition, these cultures knew their land. They took the time to observe it and remember where every single thing was—fruiting trees, underground water and habitats for certain animals. They understood the natural cycles of seasons, water and vegetation growth, and lived their lives accordingly.

I recently went on a trip to central Australia to spend time with some Aboriginal Elders. I was amazed at the detail in which they knew their land. We travelled for hundreds of kilometres through seemingly monotonous landscape, and yet the Elders could point out specific trees of significance, tiny surface springs and underground food sources.

The Aboriginal peoples of Australia, as with other Indigenous cultures, are in-tune with their land. They work in synchronicity with the land and sea—their Country—listening to what it is offering and what it needs to keep it healthy. They know when it's sustainable to take from the land and sea, and what to give back.

One other thing that the first people knew to be important was honouring spirit. Not just their own, but the spirit of all things in their environment—a healthy spirit is the key to life. Through song, dance, prayer, blessings and gifts, these Indigenous peoples honour and nourish their own spirit and that of their Country for the benefit of all.

Perhaps, one of the wisest understandings of Indigenous cultures is that they are not above their environment. They do not regard themselves as better than the trees, the animals and the landscape. They know that they have no more right to be there than anything else. All are equal.

How much we have regressed from the knowing of our ancestors!

Unlike the knowledge of current civilisations, the wisdom of Indigenous peoples was not theorised or over-intellectualised. It was about survival—plain and simple. If they were to live and ensure their children and children's children would be able to live, they had to respect the land.

On planet Earth today, there are fewer people thinking and acting like the ancestral Indigenous peoples did. Most people aren't even aware of how wise these peoples were, or how we could learn from them. Sadly, the common belief is that they were primitive, naïve and incapable of advancing like the rest of society.

We need to acknowledge that traditional custodians of the land, past and present, know how to successfully live in their environments. We need to start adopting some of their practices if we are to live on a planet that is healthy enough to continue to sustain human life.

That's where you come in. Modern Earth Healers need

to be everyday people like you and me. People who are willing to stand up and start caring for our Mother the way our ancestors did. We cannot wait for others to do it and we cannot count on our governments to do it for us.

> *The modern Earth Healer does not have to wear cloaks, live in the jungle, have tribal tattoos, or chain themself to a tree.*

He or she does not have to meditate for hours a day, or spend thousands of dollars on environmental and healing courses (although, you can do these things too if that's what makes you happy). Modern Earth Healers can do or wear whatever they like, live wherever it feels like home and enjoy themselves, as long as they are giving back to Mother Earth.

The modern Earth Healer is simply someone who cares for Mother Earth and does his or her best to reciprocate the energy She gives us. The form of energy we give back can differ greatly. It all benefits our Mother.

Though I will go into detail about specific ways each of us can help the planet in later chapters, the innate wisdom we have acquired from our ancestors should not be dismissed as an unreliable source of information for Earth healing. We all have cellular memory from when our past generations were stewards of the land and we can awaken that knowledge at will. We can all call upon that wisdom to help us become more effective at Earth healing. Furthermore, we can call on our ancestors themselves to help us to look after Mother Earth at any given time.

Most modern Earth Healers have similar qualities, including:

- giving back to the Earth (whether it's physically or metaphysically)
- making an effort to reduce their environmental footprint
- being conscious of where their food and consumables come from
- knowing the power of their money and spending it on ethical brands/stores
- appreciating the value of nature
- knowing how magical Mother Earth and all of her living creatures are
- living with less rather than accumulating as much 'stuff' as possible
- understanding that they are not above all other living things
- knowing that they do not have a right to take, hunt or kill whatever they want from nature just because they are human
- believing in a kinder, healthier planet
- taking action instead of waiting for others to take action in helping the planet
- making an effort to love all others.

Every single one of us has the power to start Earth healing. It is not difficult or necessarily arduous. Every single one of us has a responsibility to start Earth healing. As children of the Earth, we need to start being grateful for what we have been given and act accordingly.

The power of one person should not be underestimated. One person makes a difference. One person has the ability to initiate a new norm where the Earth is respected and nourished. Just as one drop can create a ripple effect across an entire lake, one person can create change that affects the entire globe.

As soon as one person takes a stance, they influence others around them. They become leaders and change-makers. They help others to see a different way of doing things and encourage these people to do the same.

Earth healing should eventually become a way of life once again, rather than a concerted effort. Looking after nature and giving back to it in return for what it gives us should become so ingrained our lifestyles that we don't even need to think about it. It should just be the 'done thing', rather than something that has to be forced.

To truly heal the Earth from its current state, the modern Earth Healer needs to be you, me and everyone else. That's how much energy we need to start giving back to Mother Earth to make her healthy again. It's the only way to sustain the human population.

It starts now—with YOU.

# Chapter 3: Mother Earth gives you everything you need to survive

Have you ever stopped to consider that Mother Earth gives you every single thing you need to survive? Every. Single. Thing. More than that actually, she gives you everything you need to have a happy, healthy life.

Food, shelter, clothes, water, air, stuff to clean your teeth with, makeup, resources to generate power, fuel, fire, places of beauty, other people, other living creatures, crystals, jewellery, musical instruments. Whatever it is you want or need, nature can provide it in some shape or form.

It blew me away when I first realised this. You see, I've grown up in a time of having pretty much everything right there for me at the shops. I never had to go and actually pick food from trees or hunt or start fires so that I could eat or cook. Whatever I wanted or needed was sitting on a shelf somewhere, most likely wrapped in plastic.

I had no idea where most stuff came from. I had no idea what things were made of or how they were made—I was completely disconnected from food and product life cycles. I was happy to accept whatever was presented to me and certainly didn't give thanks to where it came from.

The thing that first made me realise all of this was meat. As an animal lover, I became interested in how animals were treated before they ended up in butchers shops and supermarkets. What I found out saddened me to my core.

It wasn't the way the animals were actually slaughtered

(not that I like that part of the process either), it was the way that the animals were not seen as being living creatures with emotions, character and desires to enjoy their lives. These animals give their lives to provide food for us and yet they are unappreciated and treated inhumanely.

Although I'm a vegetarian, I don't actually have a problem with people eating meat—as long as the animal was treated with respect, killed without suffering (including fear), and appreciated for all that it gives to the person eating it (i.e. nutrients, nourishment and energy).

Mass produced animals are subjected to horrible conditions. Often these animals don't have any space to walk, let alone get outside, see the sunshine or smell the grass. They are pumped with hormones and chemicals and killed without a thought if they are not up to 'standard'. And most people either don't know this or don't care; others choose to be blissfully ignorant. (If you'd like to know more about this sort of thing, check out Melanie Joy's book, *Why We Love Dogs, Eat Pigs and Wear Cows*).

As a human being, I was ashamed at how we could treat other living creatures like this. Where was the compassion? Where was the love? Why were people happy to accept this in their own communities?

It made me realise that it wasn't just me that was disconnected from where our food comes from; it was the majority of people in Western society. They don't think any further than the supermarket. What has gone on behind closed doors to get products onto the shop shelves is not their problem.

Except, it kinda is—particularly meat. When we eat animals that are either mass-produced, had horrible and unhappy lives, or die in fear, we take on those denser energies. Not to mention all of the chemicals and hormones that has been fed to them during their lifetime.

When we don't pay attention to where our food and consumables come from, we don't see how the cost producing them impacts on Mother Earth. We have no emotional connection and therefore no vested interest in improving the status quo. Whatever happens 'over there' is not our problem.

Unfortunately, we can't continue to turn a blind eye. Rapidly growing populations, depleting natural resources, and less undisturbed and more contaminated natural environments, mean that to survive as a species we need to start turning things around now.

We must stop seeing ourselves as separate from the environment. How we treat it affects us—we are dependent on it. Treating Mother Earth with disrespect is treating ourselves with disrespect.

> *'How we treat ourselves is how we treat the Earth and how we treat the Earth is how we treat ourselves.'*

It can all seem very overwhelming and depressing hearing about the state of the world. You want to do something to help, but aren't sure how? Luckily, there is one very simple way to get you on track to becoming a pro-environment citizen—start appreciating what nature does for you!

Let's look at some of the key things the Earth provides for us and how these help us to live our lives well.

## Food

We all know that we need food to survive. In the developed world, the majority of people have ample food options. Not just types of foods, but brands, variations and combinations. As people are becoming more conscious of being healthy, there has also been a rise in health food products.

As much as we may try to shop for the healthiest foods to put fuel in our bodies, nobody can deny that the best food for us is the stuff straight from nature. No processing, no chemicals and no fancy marketing campaign telling us why it's the latest and greatest thing.

Why? Because these are the only substances our bodies know how to process well. Thousands of years of evolution based on all natural, seasonal foods have made our bodies super machines at breaking down those foods to extract the nutrients needed for nourishment.

Everything else? Most likely they cause pain and are difficult for your body to process. They are foreign substances that our bodies aren't quite sure what to do with and that don't contribute to any necessary bodily function. It's 'food' that probably makes you feel lethargic, bloated, gives you brain fog and makes you put on weight.

I know we are all human and we all like to indulge every now and again. I love a good red wine and I'm not here to preach that you should or shouldn't eat certain things—I'm just reminding you that some of the foods we ingest nourish our body, and others make it sick.

The good, wholesome food that comes directly from nature (without pesticides or chemicals added) sustains your bodily functions and helps you to live at your optimum potential. A diet filled with a variety of fresh, natural food will meet all of your dietary requirements.

In terms of life force energy, according to yogic tradition, the closer the food you eat was to the sun, the more life force it will give you. By that, I don't mean the food in the tallest trees, but foods that have grown with exposure to the sun; be it from fruits, nuts, or plants that have grown in the sun. To this end, the more processed a food is, the less life force energy it will have in it to nourish the person eating it.

**Water**

Water is vital for all of life—required to support all body functions, cleanse our systems and keep us at homeostasis. We also use it in nearly every aspect of our lives: cleaning, mineral production, primary production and electricity production to name a few. Most of us take water availability for granted though. And many waste it due to this.

Obviously, the Earth has plenty of water on it—70% of the Earth's surface is covered in water. So why should we appreciate it? Firstly, only 3.5% of the world's water is actually fresh. Secondly, Mother Earth's natural processes filter the water for us.

Salty, inconsumable water is picked up from the oceans via the process of evaporation, taken across to the lands we inhabit by the driving force of wind, and released as fresh, drinkable water. Then it spreads out to reach the Earth's inhabitants via creeks, rivers and streams. It's delivered to our doors.

That's pretty amazing don't you think? That we can sit back and be bought fresh water? It's free too (until governments and corporations step in). But when was the last time you stopped to appreciate this?

The bottled water industry has succeeded due to the health movement—there has been demand from people wanting to put clean, non-contaminated water into their bodies. Unfortunately, many people don't realise what this industry is doing to the environment.

Plastic bottles are one of the major sources of discarded waste and pollution. It takes three to five times the amount of water to produce a plastic bottle than the amount of water one contains. Not to mention the exploitation of Mother Nature's clever and free water cycle.

## Air

The Earth's atmosphere is made up of precisely the right mixture of gases to allow us to live. Nature's process has created a perfect blend for us humans and sustains these blended gases at suitable levels for us.

Species of trees, plants, plankton, algae and more take in carbon dioxide for us. Many of them give back oxygen for us to utilise. Nitrogen is provided for us to use in amino acids, nucleic acids and organic compounds. If the atmosphere didn't contain the correct amounts of these gases we simply could not survive.

## Shelter

So many natural materials are available to us for constructing our houses and shelters. Wood from trees is commonly used as the major structural component or 'bones' of houses, clay for roof tiles and bricks, and stone for floors and benches.

Let's not forget about the natural materials that are processed to be used in large-scale construction also. They do come from the Earth after all. Steel, for example, is a major material used when building new man-made structures, as is concrete.

Natural materials also have great insulating properties and minimise energy usage. Many people seeking to build more eco-friendly houses are now seeing the benefits of using non-manufactured resources in order to save money and live more harmoniously with their surroundings.

Some people have even turned to bio-mimicking to manage their properties. In this process the inhabitants copy the way their landscape manages the elements and they design their homes and land accordingly. They understand that Mother Nature knows the best way to manage herself, and so copying her ways is the smartest approach to looking after their property.

Our bodies need shelter from the elements also. Another

way the environment provides us with shelter is by creating materials that we can use to make clothing. Mother Nature always ensures there are things we can use to keep us warm and protected: plant materials to make fabric, animal skins (ethically sourced, of course) and naturally occurring ointments or pastes are just a few such examples.

## Medicine

Until the last 150 years or so, medicines came directly from nature. Whatever ailments we had could be cured with a natural remedy. Indigenous peoples knew (and still know) exactly what they could use from their environment to heal themselves.

Back then, any naturally occurring problem (which includes any disease or ailment that humans incur—human beings are a natural part of nature don't forget), could be addressed with naturally occurring produce.

Of course, much of this knowledge has been lost and much of the natural landscape that was home to these cures has been wiped out. Pharmaceutical companies also do a fine job at making us believe that, 1. Natural medicines don't work; 2. We need to use pills to fix problems, rather than address the cause of the problem; and 3. Good medicines need to cost lots of money.

(I do believe that man-made medicine benefits us as well. Sometimes, there are no natural alternatives for the treatment of modern diseases. However, nature has so much to offer that can help, it shouldn't be disregarded or unappreciated.)

## Recreation

It's all available to you in the great outdoors, whether it's forests to walk through, beaches to swim at, lakes to ski on, lookouts to view amazing landscapes from, mountains to climb or parks to picnic at. Most of us like to spend our holidays, weekends and spare time visiting places like this because they are free (or at least cheap) and they help us to unwind physically, mentally and emotionally, and connect in spiritually.

Mother Nature created all of these places, yet how often does she get acknowledged for doing so?

## Upliftment

'Biophillia' is a term that relates to the feeling we get when we become awe-inspired by something in the natural world. I get it whenever I see a cute creature or an animal in the wild. The fact is that nature can be incredibly uplifting for us.

Just spending time in nature does wonders for our health and state of mind. In fact, in 2012, Scientific American published an article by Deborah Franklin that shows evidence that nature reduces our anger, anxiety and pain in just three to five minutes!

There is also evidence of the natural environment improving people's memory and attention spans. An hour spent in nature is suggested to improve these brain functions by a staggering 20% according to a study by University of Michigan researchers. That's in addition to nature improving our natural creativity and increasing the sensitivity of all of our senses.

Nature also provides our physical bodies with what we need for optimal health, which equates to a happier state of mind. For example, phytoncides (substances emitted from plants and trees) and ions (charged atoms) assist various human biological functions. It is said that we build up a positive charge in our bodies from spending too much time using electronics such as our phones, computers, televisions and tablets. While positive charge may sound appealing, it's actually the opposite of what we need.

When we spend all of our time indoors, this charge has no way of escaping or neutralising. This results in a feeling of pent-up energy and anxiousness. (Considering this, it's no surprise that anxiety has become such a big problem in today's society.) When we spend time connecting with nature, however, we release some of that positively charged energy into the Earth. In return we receive naturally occurring anions (negatively charged ions) to neutralise our body's charge.

Spending time in our natural environment is also beneficial in terms of providing our bodies with fresh air that has no pollutants and which nourishes our respiratory system. That is opposed to the air in polluted places like cities that overload our bodies with toxins and put us under stress.

Walking barefoot on the Earth each day is also said to have wonderful mind and body benefits. If you've ever had foot reflexology massage, you would know that there are pressure points linked to all of the organs in your body.

Walking barefoot on natural, uneven ground ensures each of these pressure points gets due pressure applied to them. That means that each of your organs benefits when you walking around outside without shoes on.

Nowadays, many people spend their lives either indoors or with shoes on when they go outside. There is a common belief that walking without shoes outdoors is unsafe or unhealthy, but so is never walking barefoot. Some places may be contaminated or polluted with sharp materials, so you wouldn't walk there, but there are plenty of other safe places at which to walk without shoes.

In addition to the reflexology benefits of walking on the Earth, our bodies also pick up microbes that aid our bodily functions and make us feel happy. One such microbe— Mycobacterium vaccae—has been shown to mirror the effects of taking the antidepressant drug 'Prozac', by stimulating serotonin production. We benefit from these microbes each time we connect our bare skin (not just our feet) with soil, rocks, water or plants.

Spending time in the environment is also good for your spirit. The naturally high vibrational state of healthy ecosystems lifts your own vibration. You literally don't have to do anything else but sit, stand or lay there and accept the gifts coming your way.

Furthermore, being in nature has the ability to increase our ability to love and have empathy for other living creatures. Have you ever seen an animal do something cool and then fallen in love with their kind? I have! One example that comes to mind was when I saw a crow crack a seven-step, chronological puzzle in order to obtain some food. It was just brilliant!

Spending time in nature gives us that chance to see how amazing different living specimens are. All creatures are magnificent in their own way, but we miss all of that if we never take the time to observe them. Even worse, we become apathetic to the species we inhabit this Earth with and their needs.

## Wisdom

The Earth and all of its wild inhabitants have much to teach people. They don't try and go against the laws of nature. They don't worry and pine over what might happen in the future. They accept what is and move on.

Things in the wild live life in the moment and rejoice in the good times. They accept death as a part of life and they know they are part of the food chain. They listen to the world around them and work in sync with seasons and food availability.

I write a bit about animal wisdom and I am never short of insights. It's incredible how much you can learn when you start taking notice. Every different species has mastered life in some way, which if we were to adopt that wisdom, could help us in our own lives also. For example, the hummingbird lives its life following beautiful flowers and nectar. Metaphorically, this could be applied to our own lives in terms of only looking at the positives and not getting weighed down by negative thoughts or concerns. The whale is the master of self-expression, unafraid to sounds its unique voice. Again, these are qualities that we could adopt to live happier lives.

Once you realise how much animals have to teach us, you'll respect them more. I wish everyone saw how amazing all animals are so that they would protect them from harm. They are, after all, here to experience life on Earth—just like us.

All of this wisdom is available to us if we would only stop, take time out in nature, observe what is happening and contemplate all that is. When you do this, you will no longer need to seek answers from self-help books or gurus.

*As Einstein once said, 'Look deep into nature and you will understand everything better'.*

As you can see, Mother Nature does a lot for us! There are plenty of other things She does for us, of course. These are only some of the major ones.

*What other gifts from Mother Nature can you start to appreciate more in your daily life?*

The more society appreciates what nature does for us, the more everyone wants to protect it. Harping on about what people are doing wrong and how they are stupid doesn't lead to progression. But educating people to understand how amazing the environment is goes a long way.

When talking about the Earth we need to remember that we are all Mother Earth's children. Like our human mothers,

She wants us to live happy, healthy lives and to do the things we love. We don't need to spend our lives meditating or denying ourselves the things we desire. We came here to experience life on Earth as humans and that life should not be wasted—we should all be out there having fun! But have respect for her when doing it. She doesn't need us to wallow in sadness because of the way humankind has treated her. She is Gaia and she will not be destroyed! She will carry on whether humans inhabit her or not. She wants us to enjoy our time here, but needs us to understand that to really enjoy ourselves, we need to live in harmony with her.

Mother Earth wants to nurture us and she has the capability to do so if only we would stop interfering. She can't help us if we don't connect with her, use the food that she provides us and understand and appreciate what she gives us. Mother Earth urges us to take what she can give, but sustainably.

# Chapter 4: Connecting to the Earth

Developing a connection with the Earth is an important step in Earth healing. It gives us an affinity for it and allows us to listen to and understand what the Earth really needs—this is imperative for our health as human beings.

I once channelled a message from Mother Earth urging us to connect with her more:

> *'At present, the majority of people on the planet are disconnected from me. The more disconnected people are from me, the less I can help them. I need your help to start bringing people back into connection with me so that I can support them to live healthy, happy lives.*
>
> *All people need my help to survive. But I cannot help them if they won't let me. Humans (and all living creatures) are my children and I want to be able to nurture them all. Reconnecting with me gives me that opportunity.'*
> *~ Mother Earth*

It has never been more important for us to hear Her message than it is today.

## What does connecting to the Earth actually mean?

You probably hear people talking about having a connection with something every now and again, but have you stopped to think about what it means?

*A connection is an energetic resonance with someone or something that enables the exchange of energy between the two.*

A connection in no way restricts or controls the other party. Instead, it respects them and allows them to be as they are. Energy flows easily between the two.

This is in stark contrast to having an attachment to someone or something. Attachments attempt to possess and control the other party in some way. They deplete the other's energy and are dependent on them. They are not healthy for either party. Unfortunately, most relationships are based on attachment, rather than connection.

A connection with nature is an individual and personal experience. It needs to be fostered by each person in his or her own way. It needs to be felt, seen, heard and comprehended independently in order to know and appreciate it.

We are all Earth's children; we are all born with a connection with our Mother. How strong that connection is depends on us. It takes time spent in nature to re-develop and strengthen it.

A connection with Mother Earth means knowing Her. It means understanding how She functions and knowing what She needs in order for her to be healthy. It means being able to read her and identify when something is wrong.

Furthermore, a connection with Mother Earth means knowing and appreciating all that She does for us and all living creatures on the planet. It means loving, respecting and taking care of Her. Once you have developed your connection with nature, you will no longer stand by and watch people do her harm. You will become her ally, her guardian and her voice. You will become a powerful Earth Healer.

## How did we get so disconnected?

Compared with how connected our ancestors were to the land, we have diverged incredibly. There are many contributing factors as to why we have lost our connection, but a major factor is that we don't have to hunt for and gather our food anymore (we don't even know or see where it comes from!). Our current version of hunting and gathering is going to the local supermarket a putting pre-packaged food in a plastic bag.

Due to this, we no longer pay attention to natural things that affect our food supply. Rainfall, seasons, bird and animal migration times and vegetation patterns aren't a concern for us. Therefore, we have less interest in our surrounding environments. And because we aren't directly reliant on them we've become less connected to them.

Another reason for our disconnection is that we have wiped out so much of our natural environment for development. Where we once lived in close proximity to natural spaces, now we have to travel further afield to find them. We've lost the gift of being able to observe the diverse, local ecosystems around us as part of daily life.

Sadly, most of us rarely have direct physical contact with nature these days. We wear shoes so our feet don't touch the ground. We live and work in concrete jungles and are so obsessed with everything being clean and sanitised that we prevent our children from playing in dirt. All of these limit our connection with Mother Earth.

In a recent study conducted by the Nature Conservancy, it was found that only 10% of young people were spending time in nature each day. Some have little or no access to it, and some simply prefer to stay indoors and play computer games or watch television. I think the stats would be even more confronting for adults.

*How many people do you know who consciously make an effort to spend time outdoors every day? Are you one of them?*

With our lives being so busy, many people believe they don't have the time to spend in nature. It's not treated as a priority. But I bet they would if everyone understood how beneficial connecting with nature is for our minds and bodies. That's perhaps the biggest reason why society has become so disconnected with the Earth—no one appreciates how much She does for us. Until we change that, I dare to say that it will be hard to get people to re-establish their connection with nature.

## Why it's important to connect with nature

A connection with Mother Earth enables her to send you energy to rejuvenate and uplift you. As you are one of her children, she wants nothing but health and happiness for you. She wants to take care of you and establishing a connection with her enables her to do just that.

Of course, as universal laws go, there should be an exchange for the energy that Mother Earth gives us. Unfortunately, as discussed in Chapter 1, we seem to have stopped doing that on the whole. Luckily, giving back is easy and takes less effort than you might think. (The following chapters go into detail about exactly how to give back.)

*Because the Earth literally gives us energy when we connect with it, we disempower ourselves if we don't take the time to connect.*

Our bodies are designed to take in energy from the Earth—so when we don't allow this, our bodies can't work as effectively as they are designed to.

In yogic tradition, it is said that this energy is taken up through the feet and around the body through body's main energy pathways—the nadis. In Chinese medicine, these are referred to as meridians and are the energy channels that acupuncturists work with to facilitate healing.

The Earth gives us life force energy—the stuff our spirit depends on. Therefore, our spirit also depends on us being fully connected to the Earth. To deny that, denies our spirit from being happy. When our spirit isn't happy, we don't feel fulfilled. We feel like something is missing from our lives and often we can't put our finger on what that is.

Feeling unfulfilled leads to the feeling that we don't have enough. That leads to the acquisition and consumption of more and more 'stuff' in an attempt to fill the void.

Unfortunately, when our spirit is not nurtured, we never feel like we have enough, so our thirst for material possessions can never be quenched.

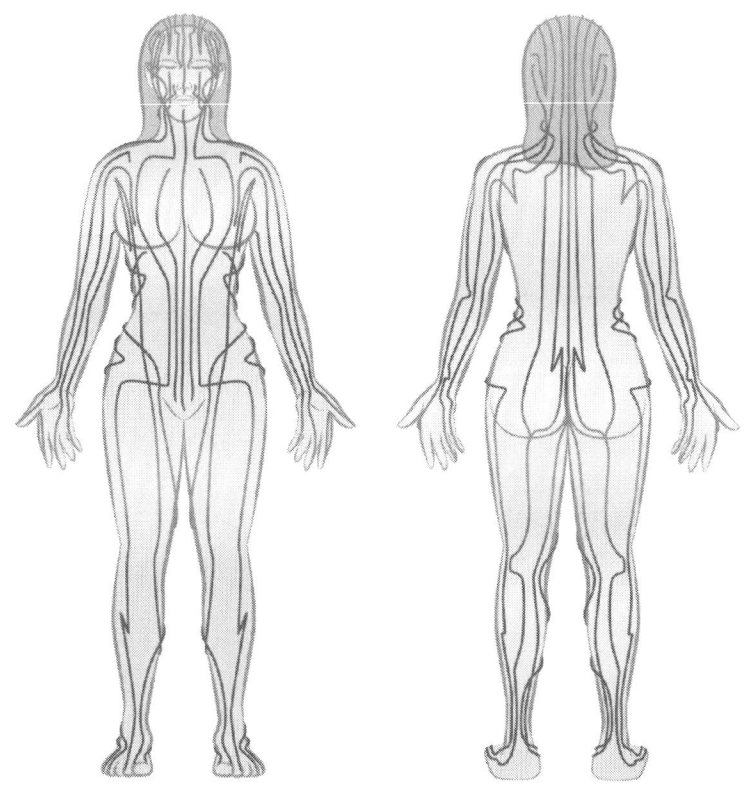

*Figure 3: The main life force energy channels in the body, known as nadis or meridians.*

When we go back and spend more time in nature, we realise how good it makes us feel. We remember that we don't actually need material possessions to make us happy. The good feelings we get when spending time outdoors cannot be topped by anything we can buy off the shelves.

A disconnection from the Earth also leaves us feeling

ungrounded. You've probably heard that being grounded is important. When we are not grounded, we are usually spending all of our time in our heads—worrying, panicking, stressing, feeling anxious and being fearful of the future. All of our energy is in the top part of our bodies, rather than being evenly dispersed throughout. We are unbalanced and have a single-minded focus. This is where we get stuck in fight or flight mode and it becomes difficult to snap out of it.

*Figure 4: Where the energy gets stuck when we overthink things and are not grounded*

When we are stuck in our heads, becoming grounded re-establishes the natural energy flows around the body. It pushes some of the energy from the mind, down and around through the rest of the body and down to our feet. Grounding your feet on the Earth literally grounds the energy in your mind and body. It calms us as we begin to synchronise with the rhythm of the Earth again.

When we are connected to Mother Earth, we can get more physical nourishment from her also. Through listening to what she is telling us, we can ask her what food or materials are best for our bodies to aid particular ailments. As we are her children, she knows exactly what we need to be healthy. Plus, she knows exactly where we can find it.

In addition, we can ask our food to nourish our bodies to it's full potential. Doing so activates the food and sends the nutrients to where we need it most. Our Indigenous ancestors did this; it enabled them to use their food efficiently; every last skerrick was used to nourish their bodies.

As an Earth Healer, having a connection with Mother Earth is vital—it enables you to listen to what she needs so that you can be of service to Her.

## How to reconnect with nature

The quickest and simplest way to connect with nature is to spend more time in it. Spend more time observing and appreciating it. Take notice of how this makes you feel. It only takes 20 minutes to really connect.

However, there are other things you can do if you'd like to connect on an even deeper level.

Firstly, if you want to achieve something—no matter what it is in life—you should set your intentions. Setting the intention pinpoints a target and starts the momentum of energy towards it. It sets up a pathway between you and your goal, and propels you towards achieving it.

Through setting clear intentions you are also telling your subconscious what you are aiming to do. Once your subconscious is on-board, it can get to work on helping you behind the scenes. It will start taking notice of things that will help you accomplish your goal and send any relevant information to your conscious mind.

Therefore, if you would like to develop a stronger connection with nature, state that. Tell your subconscious self, nature and the Universe that you would like a deeper connection with Mother Earth. Be authentic and gracious, and allow each of these energetic beings to help you on your mission.

## 8 techniques you can use to establish a connection with the Earth

### 1. Visualise your connection with the Earth

Go somewhere outdoors where there is grass, soil, sand and other natural features around you (i.e. trees, plants, ocean, or a lake). A park or even your backyard is fine. Sit or stand on the ground, feel the support of Mother Earth beneath you. (If standing, make sure you are barefoot.)

Imagine an etheric cord running from your body to deep inside the Earth. Imagine it passing through all of the layers of soil, then into the bedrock. Go as deep as you like until you feel strongly rooted into the Earth. Now, imagine a beautiful feminine, nourishing and rejuvenating energy coming back up through that cord and into your body.

Stay in that energy and notice how good it makes you feel. Let go of any stress or worries that prevent you from enjoying the moment.

2. **Connect with each one of your senses**

   **What you can see?**

   You could try noticing how many different plant species there are, or how many insects you can spot. You could take note of the slope of the land or how tall the trees are around you.

   So often, we look around without actually taking notice of what's in front of us. We give ourselves the chance to appreciate how incredibly stunning the environment is when we stop and make an effort to take in everything around us.

   **What you can hear?**

   It could be birds singing, grass rustling, waves crashing or dogs barking. There's always a symphony of sound to tune into. It will remind you that there is much happening around you at any given moment.

**What you can feel?**

My favourite thing to feel in nature is the wind in my hair and on my skin. But you could also feel the warmth of the sun, the sprinkling of rain onto your skin, or the feeling of the ground beneath your feet. Given how diverse nature is, there are a billion things to set out to feel.

**What you can smell?**

In springtime, it's wonderful to smell the flowers. No matter what the season though, there are always different things to smell. Whether it be grasses, leaves, the ocean, or even less desirable things such as a decomposing animal nearby. Using your sense of smell is just one more way of keeping you in the present moment—it also creates memories for you to visit next time you smell the same fragrances.

**What can you sense of the invisible?**

Yes, logically this fifth point when talking about our senses would be to take notice of your sense of taste, but I'm not going to suggest you eat dirt, or try to taste the leftovers in your teeth from lunch.

Being in nature is a perfect time to take notice of your sixth sense—your intuition, or higher consciousness. While here in nature, you are relaxed, have limited distractions and are in the presence of positive energy.

Quietly notice what you can sense around you in the

metaphysical world. Can you feel the elementals, such as fairies or sprites, which like to protect the environment? The traditional custodians of the land? Your spirit guides? Can you connect to the trees or the animals around you? Nature is just as abundant with unseen energies as it is with the visible ones.

Using your senses to connect with nature is so easy that you could be tricked into thinking it isn't worth the effort. Give it a go though; you will be amazed at how much it helps!

3. **Start to notice of the natural cycles of the planet**

It could be the moon—Is it waxing or waning today? Is it a full moon or new moon?

It could be the sun—Where is it sitting in the sky? What time will it rise and set tomorrow?

It could be the seasons—What is the weather doing and what foods are growing locally?

It could be wildlife—What species of fish are those? Are migratory birds in the vicinity? Are the cicadas out? What marsupials are living in those gum trees?

Taking an interest in how the natural cycles are unfolding around you leads you to becoming in sync with nature. They enable you to go with the flow of the universal forces at play, rather than trying to work against them. Most importantly, these cycles remind you that there is more to this planet than you and me.

4. **Observe how everything in nature works together to support each other perfectly**

   The sun and the oceans help to create the rain through evaporation. Rain helps the vegetation and animals grow and survive. Animals spread seeds and help fertilise the soil. The soil provides the nutrients to grow food for living things.

   Everything in the natural world serves a purpose for something else. Every single thing plays a part in the bigger picture. It is synchronicity at its finest. Perfection!

   Observing these patterns of synchronicity deepens your understanding of the environment. Once you have a deeper understanding of how it all functions with and without, you can play a bigger role in fostering the environment's health.

5. **Stand in the rain (nude for an extra kick!)**

   When was the last time you allowed yourself to stand in the rain? More to the point, when was the last time you allowed yourself to enjoy the feeling of standing in the rain? Maybe it's not since you were a child.

   The feeling is incredibly revitalising and cleansing. If you're in a bad mood, intentionally standing in the rain will wash it all away. It reminds us of our inner child (remember her/him?) and is one of the cheapest and most effective ways to lift our spirits and feel like new.

   Standing in the rain instantly makes you realise that you

are part of the natural environment; that you are ingrained in its systems, cycles and rhythms. If this Earth wisdom doesn't make you feel connected, I don't know what will.

## 6. Acknowledge when you see something wonderful in nature

Let Mother Earth know that you are paying attention; and that you see the amazingness that She is capable of! The more you start to appreciate and focus on these, the more cool things you will notice. It will deepen your connection with Her and all that surrounds you will.

## 7. Acknowledge the energy you take from Mother Earth throughout your daily life

In order to live, you need to take energy from the Earth. It's an inevitable fact of life. Whether it's food, life force energy, water or any other form of energy, you depend on it for your survival.

Acknowledging that you are taking energy from the environment serves as a good way to connect with it. This connection increases your awareness about what the environment does for you and the impact you have on in it. Once you understand how much you take, you can consider how you will give back in return.

## 8. Write a list of all that you love about nature

When you write from your heart you instantly connect—so writing down all the things you love about nature will have you connected to them and Mother Nature in no time! What's great is that you can do this from anywhere. Even if you're not in nature at the time the connection is as powerful.

Connecting with nature is not only good for your mind, body and spirit; it's good for Mother Earth too. If you want to become the most powerful Earth Healer you can be, connecting with Her is the first step.

# Chapter 5: Embracing the feminine

As human beings, an important part of healing the Earth is embracing our feminine energy. Our ancestors embraced their feminine energy as much as they did their masculine. But in modern life, we have placed a much higher value on masculine energy, which leaves us unbalanced, destructive and reckless.

As a society, we need to start honouring feminine energy again in order to start taking care of the Earth properly. The more we align with the feminine, the more we develop and affinity for Mother Earth and therefore become a voice for Her. In doing so, we are able to communicate what She needs and protect her from more damage.

Increasing our feminine energy levels opens us up to our natural Earth healing abilities. It gives us the capacity to give back. It's the feminine side of us that seeks to help, heal and care for anything in need. It's the side that protects others and us and wants all to grow and prosper.

Feminine energy is calm, and nurturing. It calls for us to rest, take stock of our lives and listen to our inner voice. This is in contrast to masculine energy that is always on the go, never rests and continually tries to achieve—it gets things done and conquers. While feminine energy allows, masculine energy forces.

*Don't be mistaken; feminine energy is by no means weak. It is fiercely passionate. It is powerful, unwavering and*

> *unshakable. It holds its power by sitting in stillness and allowing whatever is meant to be, be. Its presence alone commands authority—it doesn't need to push anything or anyone else down to be powerful. It does not enter into battle and it is never defeated.*

Feminine energy accepts and it receives. It does not chase after anything and it connects to things and people rather than attaching to them. It does not buy into fear or scarcity. It is driven by the heart and dwells in the creative mind.

Masculine energy on the other hand, is forever moving and chasing after things. It fights, it gains and loses power, it forces and it takes energy from other people and things. It is driven by ego and the analytical mind.

We are told from a young age that to be successful, you need to receive top marks in school, be great at sport, earn lots of money and work in positions of power, no matter what the cost. These are all masculine targets. To achieve these things, we disregard the part of us that tells us we need to rest more, have a healthy diet, be spontaneous and have fun.

The problem with being so masculine is that you are never satisfied. There is always more to accomplish, more to earn and more to own. You think that you'll be happy 'when …'. You think you'll be happy as soon as you achieve that next milestone; but sadly it's never enough.

The dominance of masculine energy in our society is one of the main reasons for consumerism, materialism, capitalism, people being disconnected from the Earth and the destruction of the environment. We never would have come to this point if we were all more balanced and listened to our feminine. We never would have fallen out of harmony with nature.

Happiness comes from being balanced. From achieving goals, but also taking time out to enjoy your life. Just like the infamous yin and yang symbol, balance requires both masculine and feminine energies working in sync.

Feminine energy is no better than masculine energy, or vice versa, and both are necessary to live fulfilling lives. Problems occur when one becomes more dominant than the other, which sadly is the case for most people today.

It doesn't matter which gender you are. All humans require *masculine and feminine* energy to be happy and healthy. For the vast majority of us, we need to step up our feminine for that to occur.

We need to embrace the feminine more so that we have the capacity to nurture not only ourselves, but the Earth also. When we are so caught up on getting things done and ticking things off our to-do lists we leave no space for stopping, listening and taking care of anything.

To embrace the feminine, we need to slow down. We need to slow down so that we can once again become in sync with the gentle rhythm of Mother Earth. When we do, we can feel at one with her again and be calmed by her soothing, soft hum (which is always present, whether we tune into it or not). In return, we can give her what she needs.

## 10 benefits of embracing your feminine energy

Mother Earth's energy is the ultimate feminine energy—nurturing, loving and rejuvenating. The more we connect with her, the more we are able to embrace our own feminine energy. Whether you are a man or woman, there are so many benefits to embracing your feminine energy:

1. **You become calmer**

    When things don't go your way, you realise that it's not the end of the world. Your stress levels drop because you aren't just focused on what you need to get done, and whether things are going your way that day. You are able to see the big picture in situations and value your down time as much as your 'getting things done' time.

2. **You start to enjoy the simpler things in life**

    Whether it's spending time with your pets, reading a book, or playing with your kids, you realise that these are the precious moments in life. The ones you can't put a value on. When you embrace your feminine, it isn't just that you slow down enough to be able to do these things more often, you're able to actually enjoy them because you are more present.

    When ruled by masculine energy, your mind would have only been focused on the things you needed to get done, preventing you from noticing what's happening around you. When you embrace your feminine, you are able to take stock of your surroundings and see the beauty in life.

It could be blooming flowers, people in love or perfect weather; all stuff that is free for us to enjoy and incredibly uplifting when we take the time to be with it.

### 3. Your health and happiness become the number one priority

You realise that you can't really help anyone else unless you look after yourself. Once you start doing that, you become lighter, more clear-headed and more efficient. You actually start to enjoy life more. Once you see the benefits of really looking after yourself, you'll never want to go back to your old ways.

### 4. You have more love to give

When you balance your feminine and masculine energies, you become better at only giving of yourself that which is available and sustainable to give. Because you ensure you aren't draining yourself, you can actually offer more. It may mean you have to say 'no' to helping other people sometimes, but when you do offer your assistance you'll be offering it from a happier, more effective place.

### 5. You become more creative

Perhaps you'll become more interested in photography, or online media or poetry. Whatever it is, you'll start to find creative things more fulfilling. I was never any good at art or drawing at school so I'd pretty much switched that side of myself off, but I've come to learn that there's so many different ways of being creative. Now I love to explore different methods of creativity because I really enjoy having a creative outlet. At the moment, I really love digital media.

6. **You live in the moment more**

   Instead of being so focused on what lies ahead—or what you should have done better—you can relax and focus on what's in front of you. You are able to let things go more easily and accept that you are wherever you are in that present moment.

7. **You become more contented with your life**

   Because you are less motivated by what you want to acquire and achieve, you are able to start appreciating the things you already have. You realise that perhaps you don't need all those things you thought you did and, in fact, your life is pretty good just as it is. What a gift!

8. **You become more empathetic towards others**

   When we are balanced and calm, we start to recognise that we are not the centre of the Universe and can accept that other people are no better or worse than us. We are more open to seeing things from other people's perspectives and can put ourselves in their shoes. We can also open our hearts to them more easily and can show them respect, no matter what their circumstance.

9. **You become less materialistic**

   When we embrace our feminine energy, we start to value

the things that you can't put a price on, so we care less for acquiring material possessions. It doesn't mean we want for nothing, but we are less obsessed with filling our lives with 'stuff'. We wise up to the fact that material possessions aren't the things that make us happy.

10. **You want the best for all**

    Life is no longer a competition. When you embrace your feminine, you start recognise the best in others. You start to care for everyone's wellbeing, animals included. Your ego subsides and instead of it always being about 'you', it becomes about 'us'.

## 10 ways to embody your sacred feminine

Everyone already has a feminine aspect within himself or herself, but it's likely that it's supressed. We can bring out our feminine sides out at will by carrying out a few simple practices. The following are some examples of things you can do today to start embodying your sacred feminine more.

1. **Spend time in nature (of course!)**

    Spending time in nature will naturally raise your feminine energy, not only because Mother Earth's energy is feminine and you are more exposed to it, but because you take the time to slow down. Spending time in nature affords you time to rest, rejuvenate and bask in Her natural beauty.

2. **Honour your inner child**

   Play, do the things you always wanted to do as a kid. Those are the things that really fulfil you and nourish your femininity. Most of us get too serious and boring as adults. Serious and boring drains our energy. Acting like a kid fills us with joy and harmony. It reconnects us with the parts of ourselves that don't need routine, responsibility or authority.

3. **Slow down**

   You really don't need to get all of that stuff done. Don't run yourself into the ground so much that your body will make you physically ill just so that you will stop. Embody your inner Bob Marley and relax.

4. **Allow yourself to be vulnerable**

   Pull down those walls. Let people see who you really are. Be yourself and say what you really think. I know society encourages to suck it up and be tough, but that really doesn't get us anywhere. The more we deny how we really feel, the more emotional baggage we carry around. That ends up creating mental and physical issues for us; it ultimately prevents us from enjoying life.

   Genuinely strong people actually allow themselves to be vulnerable. They know that it might be uncomfortable to do so, but they step up to the plate and do it anyway. Why? Because that's what they have to do to be authentic, and power comes from authenticity.

5. **Seek more creativity**

   There's so many different ways to be creative. You don't have to be great at the traditional arts. You could redecorate your house or garden, take up a new style of cooking, do a design course, scribble in a journal or even write a book! The possibilities are endless. All you need to do is find the creative method that floats your boat and you won't need to force yourself to do it. You'll do it because you love it and it makes you happy.

6. **Make time for fun**

   I know life is busy. I know there are so many things you need to get done. But none of it will make you feel as good as having a deep belly laugh. Having fun is so important for our health. It decreases stress levels and lifts our spirits. The thing is though; you have to make it a priority. It so easily slips down the list of things to do as soon as we get busy. If there's one thing you do for yourself today, let it be having fun. It is good for every level of your being, as well as everyone and everything around you.

7. **Take up yin yoga**

   If you've never tried it before, do yourself a favour! It feels so incredibly amazing. Yin yoga is mostly floor-based positions, each held for a longer period of time. It is much gentler on the body than other forms of yoga so it is suitable for all fitness levels.

Yin yoga is calming and allows you to stretch out areas that may never have been stretched in your adult life. You will walk out feeling blissful.

8. **Forget whatever you have planned and do something you feel like doing instead**

    Call in sick to work. Cancel your appointments. Do something that nourishes your spirit. The world won't stop without you. We need to do more of what we love and less of what doesn't light us up. It's not only good for us to do it; it's good for the planet.

9. **Don't block your sensitivity**

    I know all about this one. I hid how sensitive I really was for most of my life. It can be painful and uncomfortable to be sensitive, but it's also a gift. Our sensitivity enables us to feel into what is happening around us and understand what is needed to make it better. Our sensitivity is what makes us fantastic healers. The more we acknowledge it and listen to it, the deeper we can heal and help others to heal themselves.

10. **Get out of your head**

    The majority of us spend our lives 'in our heads'. We think about what we are going to eat next, conversations we just had, what movies we'd like to see, who we think is a jerk, etc. The problem is that spending so much time in our heads makes us unbalanced and blocks the flow of feminine energy.

In addition to spending time in nature, we can get out of our heads by breathing deeply, with equally long inhales and exhales, resting more, avoiding stimulants and meditating. We can also physically move to get the energy out of our head and flowing more around the rest of our body. Walking for 20 minutes, doing star jumps, shaking off your entire body, stomping and running are just a few ways to do that.

Embracing our feminine energy will make us all more powerful Earth Healers. Not only does it align us more with Mother Earth's energy (so we can tune into her more and help her out), it makes us all happier. That's a pretty good gift to the rest of the world!

# Chapter 6: Lessening your environmental impact

Before we talk about how we can start giving back to Mother Earth, we should really look at how we can take less from her in the first place. The less we take, the less that needs healing, the greater total positive impact we will have when we start Earth healing.

Every single living creature on this planet has some sort of impact on its environment. It's unavoidable. Humans have, by far, the largest impact—which is grossly unnecessary. Although we can't completely avoid having an impact, we can reduce our environmental footprint as much as possible.

I'd like to start by first saying that I am by no means the most eco-friendly person living on the planet. I do not have zero waste, I drive a car and, sometimes, I'll get sucked in by a good marketing campaign that coerces me into buying junk I don't need. There are plenty of other people out there doing more incredible, amazing things to lessen their environmental footprint than me.

What I am, though, is someone who is committed to continually improving and reducing my impact little-by-little, as time goes on. Because these little things count. And over time, each little act adds up to a much more eco-friendly lifestyle.

I encourage you to start out making small choices to help the environment whenever you can. It could be saying 'no' to plastic bags and drinking straws, for example. After a while, those choices become habits. With these habits as part of our daily life we can focus our attention on a few other little things we can do to help nature. Then those things become habit, and so on.

Before you know it, you'll be an eco-warrior. The best thing is, the more choices you make to help the environment, the more you become aware of other things you can do. You might find wonderful eco brands that have a wide range of products and solutions to things you never even realised were a problem. Or you might start meeting other like-minded people who have environmental wisdom to impart to you.

If you want to go all out and switch to a completely environmentally friendly lifestyle overnight, go ahead. Don't be surprised, though, if you find it difficult to sustain that lifestyle. Not to mention the cost of doing it. Rapidly equipping yourself with a broad range of re-usable, recycled or biodynamic tools can be an expensive task. Slowly acquiring these things over time is more manageable.

Trying to do everything all at once can also lead to overwhelm. As someone who can become obsessive and anxious over whatever I set my mind to, I have experienced this firsthand. Just remember that every little step in the right direction is progress. It's okay to not be perfect right from the get go—just do what you can, when you can.

## Find your 'Why?'

In my opinion, the easiest way to find your commitment to

the cause of reducing your ecological footprint is to understand what motivates you personally.

For me, a huge motivator is seeing the impact we have on animals. Witnessing turtles that have starved to death after swallowing plastic bags, or the remains of birds that have eaten plastic waste, was all the motivation I needed to change the way I live.

Your motivation to help the planet could be to ensure your children, and your children's children, are able to live in a healthy environment. Maybe it's to protect the area you grew up in that was always abundant with wildlife and beautiful trees. Finding your own motivation brings caring for the environment 'home'. It becomes relatable. No longer will caring for Mother Earth be some 'out there' thing that doesn't really affect you—instead you will feel compelled to act.

## Reducing your physical environmental footprint

On a day-to-day basis, there are three general rules to reduce your environmental footprint—use less, produce less waste and natural is always better. It doesn't matter whether you're at home, at work, or out and about doing your thing, these general rules will ensure that you are kinder to the environment.

Use less of everything—water, energy, materials, food, cosmetics—everything. It doesn't matter what it is, a lot of energy has been used to produce and transport it to you. Using less will reduce how much you take from the environment. Take shorter showers, walk or ride instead of driving, be less frivolous with consumables like toothpaste and more mindful about the size of your meals. Every little bit helps.

Aim to generate less waste by avoiding single use items, upcycling what you have or that someone gives you, donating things you don't need to those who do and buying better quality/long-lasting products. And avoid packaging wherever you can, especially plastic packaging. Plastic is the king of waste and root of all evil.

Use, grow and buy natural products that are better for the environment—they won't cause the environment harm at end of their product life. Natural materials can be broken down by nature and utilised for their nutrients. They actually give something back to the environment, unlike man-made products that either release harmful, toxic waste or cannot be broken down for thousands of years. Of course, I'm only talking about sustainably sourced natural products. Any that required the destruction of native forests or animal habitats are not worth the cost. Luckily, there's a rise in the availability of sustainably and ethically sourced products these days.

## 25 practical ways you can reduce your physical impact on the planet

1. **Stop caring as much about how things look**

    How much energy goes into making sure your lawns are well kept, your hair is perfect, you're wearing the latest fashions, you've adequately decorated your house for whichever holiday it is, etc.? Fuel for mowers and whipper snippers, electricity for hair dryers, chemicals for dyes, materials and waste water for clothes, plastic and single use items for decorations. It all adds up.

I'm not saying to avoid these things altogether, but we could all let things slide just a little bit more. Instead of getting your lawns done every two weeks, make it three. Get your hair done less often and mix and match your clothes a bit more. Additionally, wear your clothes more than once before washing them. Tiny efforts like these all make a difference over time.

2. **Buy second-hand clothes**

Did you know that only about 20% of clothes get recycled worldwide? That's a whole lot of threads being sent to landfill! Did you know that the production of clothes is a major cause of water pollution across the globe? The impacts of the fashion industry can be lessened every single time you chose second-hand clothes over new ones. And there's always the added benefit of saving you a wardrobe-load of money!

3. **Have less kids**

The size of the human population is by far the biggest cause of environmental degradation on planet Earth. The more people there are, the more demand there is for land and consumables. Population control needs to be on the agenda when we talk about saving the planet. We already have trouble sustaining the current population. The more we grow, the less ability the Earth has to support us.

I'm not suggesting that you should not have children at all, but deciding to have one or two less than originally planned for the sake of the Earth should be a major consideration. Having one less child will help the environment more than another other initiative stated here by a long shot!

4. **Don't fall for the old biodegradable bag trick**

    Most biodegradable bags still take a very long time to degrade. During that time, they can cause all the same negative impacts that plastic bags do (such as pollution, clogging up waterways and causing harm to wildlife). The best option is always re-usable bags.

5. **Use cloths to dry your hands after you wash them**

    If a cloth is not available, don't be afraid to use the clothes you are wearing (remember, we need to care less about what we look like). Or let them drip dry. Do we really need to waste paper or electricity on drying our hands? Imagine how much we could save if every office and public toilet said 'no' to paper towel and hand dryers!

6. **Borrow things from friends, family and neighbours**

    When did we become a society in which everyone needed to own everything? Owning everything is costly and takes up a lot of space. There is nothing wrong with borrowing items, at least for tasks you do infrequently. Doing so also ensures the borrowed item is used more over its lifespan, making it an efficiency initiative as well.

7. **Trade items**

    Instead of spending money on buying new products, you could swap with other people. Maybe they have something you want and you have something they want? Swapping not only helps the environment by reducing the demand for materials and processing, it also helps by reducing the amount of waste you produce. Instead of putting that item you no longer need into landfill, give it to someone who has a use for it (and vice versa).

8. **Buy locally made products**

    Buying locally not only supports your local economy, it also helps nature by reducing the amount of energy used through transportation. Often buying locally also prevents the need for as much packaging.

9. **Grow your own**

    Now, I'm not a green thumb but I still manage to grow a few veggies. If I can do it, you can too! You don't even need a big yard these days. You can buy portable veggie plots for inside or out. It's rewarding and I think the food even tastes better!

    Planting certain species, like lavender and citronella, can also help with keeping mozzies and flies away.

10. **DIY cleaning products**

    There's plenty of information out there about using standard household materials to create cleaning products for the home and for personal use. Shampoos, conditioners, toilet cleaners, glass cleaners—it can all be made simply and cheaply. Much can be made from bi-carb soda and apple cider vinegar.

    Using products like these not only helps by limiting the amount of chemicals you release into the environment, it also reduces packaging and waste generation. Again, it will also save you money!

11. **Hang your clothes out**

    How many people these days just throw their laundry in the dryer after it has been washed instead of hanging it out? I know I have been guilty of doing this a few times. Using the wind and sun to dry your clothes will save you in energy and sterilise your clothes with UV rays.

12. **Buy organic**

    Buying organic means less chemicals going into the environment and into you. The more demand we create for organic food and materials, the more variety there will be and the cheaper it will become.

13. **Eat less red meat**

    Being a vegetarian, I couldn't help but slip this in. Eating less red meat reduces the demand, meaning less land is needed for livestock, less greenhouse gas is generated and less energy is wasted through transportation. The process of producing beef, in particular, is a very inefficient.

## 14. Support environmental organisations who do good work

It doesn't have to be support in the form of financial donations either. Sharing information or becoming an advocate for these organisations is a great help also. Or you can volunteer your time and skills, meet likeminded people and learn a thing or two.

## 15. Spend your money on ethically sourced materials

In our society, nothing speaks louder than dollars. Where and what you spend your money on is the best way to get companies to listen to what you want. The more you buy products that are the kinder to the environment, the cheaper they can be made available through economies of scale.

## 16. Pick up rubbish in public places

Yes, I know it's not technically *your* environmental footprint that you're reducing here, but you are helping the environment and its creatures, which is the aim of the game. Plus, if you don't do it, no one else is likely to.

Picking up rubbish and being seen doing it is a great way to create change in your local neighbourhood—it lets others know that some people actually care that waste has been discarded there. This will also deter people from discarding waste there in the first place. When other people see you collecting random rubbish encourages them to pick up rubbish also. People tend to hate being the odd one out, but if you make picking up rubbish the 'done thing', no one will bat an eyelid when they see others doing it. Lead by example and others will feel safe enough to do it too.

## 17. Support your local environment

Learn what types of animals you have locally. What do they like to eat and where do they like to live? Learn about the different kinds of trees in the area. The more you know, the more inclined you will be to protect the environment and contribute to its health.

As an added bonus, you can teach others what you have learnt so that they create a vested interest in saving it also.

## 18. Use websites and organisations that allow you to advertise what you are looking to discard/pickup

Instead of sending perfectly good items to landfill, or shopping for brand new, make the most of websites and organisations (for example, Freecycle.org) that allow you advertise items that you would otherwise discard in landfill. And use local drop-off points for items that shouldn't make their way to landfill at all, like printer cartridges, through providers such as Planet Ark.

## 19. Ease up on the sunscreen

The non-natural ones, anyway. All those chemicals in

sunscreen end up in the water when you go swimming. Have you been to the beach or lake lately and noticed the film of sunscreen on the surface of the water? That's us humans polluting right there!

Recent scientific studies have even shown that sunscreens are having a harmful effect on the Great Barrier Reef and no doubt other reefs around the world. When we release unnatural chemicals into the environment, no matter how it is done, we create a negative impact. Plants, animals and ecosystems are not designed to cope with such things. It harms them.

It's important to mention that even the Cancer Council of Australia—in the country where sun cancer is the most prevalent in the world—lists sunscreen as the last option for protection from the sun. Wear a hat or sun-shirt, or go into the sun during times of less extreme UV levels to reduce your sunscreen consumption. Don't forget, some time in the sun is good—it gives us vitamin D and helps us to be healthy physically and mentally.

## 20. Only disturb as much land and vegetation as necessary for your home

There's no need to clear all the vegetation on your block. Leave some places undisturbed to allow the area to function as naturally as possible. Remember, all the species of vegetation, ground cover and rocks are there because they thrive there. Keeping them there will help with drainage, erosion, local wildlife, etc. Maintaining existing ecosystems will assist with the overall health of your property.

## 21. Allow wildlife to visit your property

Every animal plays a part in the natural cycles and ecosystems around your house. Allowing them to stay actually benefits you in terms of living in a healthier environment. Leave as much habitat for them as possible, place a birdbath in the yard, plant native species, hang possum boxes. We have no more right to this land than any other living thing.

## 22. Utilise renewable energy wherever you can

Solar, wind, hydro—they're all fantastic, natural sources of energy. Even if you can't utilise these directly at your property, you can elect to purchase renewable energy from your electricity provider. The more we support renewables, the cheaper it will become and the less demand there will be for fossil fuels. And when if you're renovating or building, incorporate these power solutions into your project from the beginning.

## 23. Eat-in rather than take-away

Spend five extra minutes eating in at your local café or restaurant rather than taking away. It saves in packaging and will give you a chance to relax for a few minutes.

## 24. Buy in bulk

Buying consumables in bulk saves on packaging. Find a

friend or family to share with if you find there is too much for you to consume in bulk.

## 25. Make your own paper bin liners and wrapping paper

Instead of using plastic bags for bins and single-use wrapping paper, use newspaper that would otherwise go straight in the bin. There are instructional guides of how to do it all over the internet.

### It's more than just a physical thing

Most of the time, when people talk about reducing their environmental footprint, they are only referring to their physical impact; land disturbance, waste, pollution, etc. Not many people acknowledge the metaphysical impact we also have on the world around us. (Metaphysics can be described as being beyond the physical or visible.) And just as we have a physical impact on the planet, we also have a metaphysical impact. In the simplest of terms, people who are unhealthy, unhappy or negative, place a heavier load on the environment. Their energy is denser and they operate at a lower vibrational state.

People who have a heavier metaphysical impact act as energy sinks and draw down on energy from the space around them. They change their environment into a more negative one and they slow the pace of activity. Essentially, they drag everything else around them down.

This is in contrast to someone who is energetically lighter. They are healthier, happier and more positive. They lift the energy of the people and places around them. They see solutions, are more loving and empathetic, and they are in a position to help others.

Think what I am saying is a bit far-fetched? Just think about how much impact someone in a bad mood can have on you, the people around you and everyone they come into contact with. You could turn up at work in the best of moods, singing to yourself and feeling good about life, and then in walks crabby Marie.

Marie hates her job and, the rumour is, her husband as well. This morning she's extra cranky. She's had a fight with her husband and she's got PMS. She finds that someone in the office has used her special coffee cup and she loses it. She swears at the empty cupboard, then swears at you and then everyone else she walks past.

Now you feel a bit crappy. Marie has reminded you that your world is not all that great either. You've got to finish that tedious report by the end of the day, and to top it all off, you've got to get an embarrassing lump on your bum checked out by the doctor after work. Your day sucks!

Thanks Marie!

People operating at lower vibrational states impact us all the time. You can't see the energy they take in from—and give out into—their environment, but you can definitely feel it! Our metaphysical state impacts the space around us (including natural spaces) as much as it impacts other people. One metaphysically heavy person brings the rest of the world down, even if only a smidgen. But we are not separate from the Earth and if people are unhappy and unhealthy, the Earth is unhappy and unhealthy. We can't ignore the metaphysical health of the planet. If we truly want to heal the world, we need to heal the metaphysical energy of the world too.

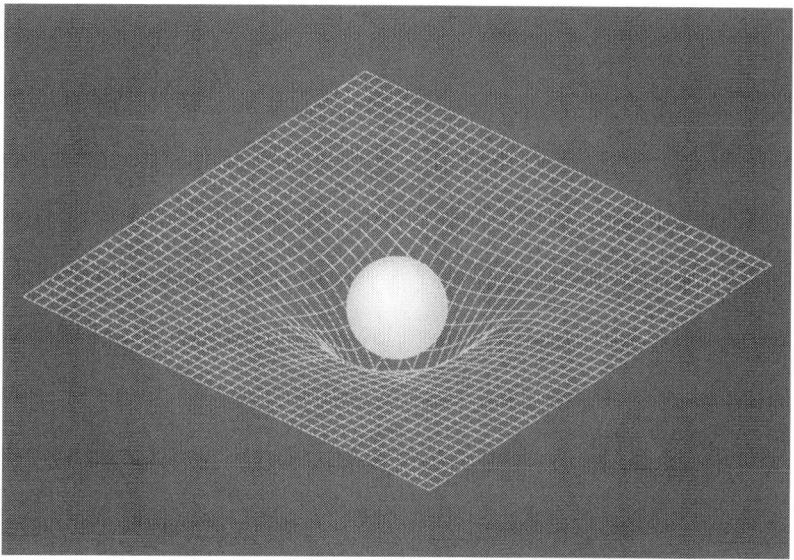

*Figure 5: A depiction of how we draw down the energy around us when we are negative, angry, unhappy, unhealthy or operating at a lower frequency. Imagine the ball is a human in a particular environment.*

We need to take responsibility for our energetic imprint on the rest of the world. We need to acknowledge that we do have an impact on others and the environment. Enough of everyone wallowing in his or her own sorrow! It's time we realise we are all connected and we have a responsibility to society to look after our own wellbeing.

It's important to reduce our metaphysical impact because we need to be positive and able to look outside of ourselves in order to reverse the damage we've done to the planet.

The Earth needs people who care and who are able to take action. We need people who can see solutions to problems, rather than dead ends and doom and gloom.

We can all lift our metaphysical state and have less of a negative impact on the world around us whenever we make an effort to. Keeping yourself healthy and joyous, and nourishing your spirit, all lessens our collective metaphysical load. In short, looking after us helps the entire planet!

## Reducing your metaphysical environmental footprint

The three general rules to lighten your energetic load on the planet are to nourish your mind, nourish your body and nourish your spirit. Of course, they are all intertwined, so doing one helps the others also. In short, anything that naturally lifts you up, makes you feel good and is healthy for you lightens your energetic load on the planet.

## 25 things you can do to reduce your energetic impact on the planet

1. **Listen to one of your favourite albums**

    Most people understand the uplifting effects of music, but it's often not a go-to solution when we are feeling low. Your favourite music does wonders for you. You like it for a reason—it speaks to your unique vibration and lifts it.

2. **Do something fun**

    There's no need to take life so seriously all the time! We

seem to have lost sight of this in our hectic lives. Having fun is super important to keeping healthy and having a positive mindset. You should know what it is that you enjoy. Maybe it's roller-skating, or perhaps it's catching waves. If you find it hard to think of what brings you joy, simply think back to when you were a child. What did you love doing then?

3. **Get an energetic healing**

   If you're not into spirituality this could be a big leap of faith for you, but they energetic healings are beneficial. Energetic healings clear out some of the gunk from our energy fields that we carry around with us. This stuff weighs us down and makes us feel flat or depressed. Releasing these energies can instantly make you feel on top of the world!

   There are many different forms of energetic healing; reiki and shamanism are two such examples.

4. **Spend time with animals**

   Animals are incredible healers. Their light vibration has an uplifting effect on everything around them. I studied animal assisted therapy for a little while and was stunned to see the extensive, scientifically proven health benefits that come from spending time with animals. Anything from reducing blood pressure and the risk of heart attack, to increased memory and empathy. All animals really are magnificent!

5. **Spend time with friends**

   Prioritise spending time with friends. Go out and talk rubbish. Have a laugh. Complain about your partners. It will help you to feel re-energised and positive. Life's too short not to enjoy it every now and again.

6. **Watch something funny**

   YouTube is full of funny videos. It doesn't matter what tickle your sense of humour, you'll find something on there to have you laughing in no time. And of course, there are always your favourite funny movies to watch.

7. **Dance**

   Be as uncoordinated as you like. It doesn't matter how you look, all that matters is that you enjoy yourself. It will help you to loosen up and lift your mood. Plus, it's a form of exercise so it will benefit your body too.

8. **Exercise**

   Do anything to get to blood pumping. It could be a walk, a run, going to the gym or playing sport. Exercise is so important for keeping your body working the way it is designed to. It keeps the energy moving, helps you to sweat out toxins, clears your respiratory system and gets the endorphins flowing. Exercise is essential to living a happy life!

9. **Eat less junk**

   The more chemicals and toxins you put into your body,

the harder it is for your body to perform as it should. Junk food affects our respiratory, digestive, cardiovascular and central nervous systems, as well as our skin and bones. It leaves us feeling worse than before. You don't have to eliminate these foods completely from your diet, but eating less junk will help you to feel better.

## 10. Meditate

Even if you think you don't know how, make sure you meditate. There is no wrong way to do it. Basically, just sit in silence for at least 15 minutes with your eyes closed. Instead of focusing on all the things you need to get done, allow your mind to rest. It will help you relax, gain clarity and re-centre yourself for the day.

## 11. Don't partake in things you know won't make you happy

Why waste your time and energy (and often money) doing things that will leave you feeling scared or down? For me, that's scary movies. Do yourself a favour and spend your time doing something that uplifts you instead. It will be better for your mind, body and spirit (and everyone in your proximity).

## 12. Dream of how you'd like your life to be

You know that amazing feeling you get when you daydream about all the things you would do if you had more time or money? Why not do it more often rather than focusing on all the worries in your life? Make it as detailed as you can. What colour is that car you want? Where exactly is the house you aim to own one day?

You might be surprised at what opportunities come your way when you start doing this. I see it as a way of co-creating our futures.

## 13. Take a break or go on a holiday

You may feel like you are too busy or don't have the funds to take a break from your everyday life, but it's so important to do it every now and again. We all need to take time out to re-set and re-evaluate our lives. Maybe you need to let go of something, or perhaps you need to put more energy into different aspects of your life. When you are busy all the time it's hard to see things from a higher perspective. We need breaks to work out what change is needed for us to be the happiest and healthiest versions of ourselves.

## 14. Put yourself first for once

If you are reading this book, chances are you are a natural nurturer. That's a beautiful thing, but it quite commonly leads people like us to put everyone else ahead of ourselves. When we don't prioritise our own needs, we can become depleted. Then we have no energy to help anyone. Look after yourself and you will be available to help others more.

## 15. Spend time in nature

*Mother Nature is the world's best healer.*

Hopefully you'll get a good understanding of this by the time you finish reading this book. I urge you to go and spend just 20 minutes in nature. Notice how wonderful it makes you feel. Once you realise how good it is to connect with Mother Nature, make it part of your regular routine.

### 16. Stop what you're doing and have a rest

Often when we think of being healthy, we think of getting out there and being active. Many people don't realise that resting is just important for your health as doing exercise. When we rest, we allow our body to repair and get rid of the things we no longer need. If we are always on the go, all our energy is used through movement. Resting allows us to refresh, regroup and rejuvenate.

### 17. Treat yourself to a massage or a spa day

Besides the relaxation benefits of this, massages and other such treatments help our bodies to function better. They help release emotional blockages, knots and toxins and re-establish the natural flow of energy throughout the body. That's a good enough excuse for me! How about you?

### 18. Stretch

Stretching can feel so amazing if you haven't done it for a while. It usually slips off the daily to-do list but it shouldn't be forgotten. Stretching helps to release built-up tension and helps with circulation. It also helps to keep us flexible and agile. If you want to feel great all round, stretching is imperative.

## 19. Eat nourishing food

Healthy food keeps you vitalised and functioning at maximum capacity. There's no better gift for your body. Ensuring you are meeting all your dietary requirements and having a balanced diet will keep you feeling energised and ready to take on the world.

## 20. Wear a scent that you love

Do you realise that scents can uplift you? There's no need to save your favourites for special occasions either. Using your favourite perfume or essential oil for to give you a little lift when you need it is worth it!

## 21. Wear an outfit that makes you feel good

Make up an occasion to get dressed up and head out. Sometimes, when we get caught up in the hustle and bustle of daily life, we can give up on trying to look and feel great. Now, I'm not one for fashion, but I do know how great it makes me feel when I wear something I love. This one simple act can change your mood completely.

## 22. Donate to a charity you truly support

My favourite charities are all organisations that help animals (I have so much respect for Animals Australia and Edgars Mission, to name a couple), but yours can be anything that warms your heart. You know what causes you are passionate about. Supporting such organisations will not only help them to do their work, it will also help you to feel good. Giving from the heart is one of the most uplifting things we can do.

### 23. Take the time to think about your best qualities and why you are awesome

It's really important to remind yourself about your good qualities and gifts. These can sometimes be forgotten when dealing with everything the outside world throws at us. Knowing who we are and what we have to offer keeps us strong and unshakable. If we are to make the world a better place we need more kind and unshakable people standing in their power!

### 24. Go for a swim in the ocean

One of my personal favourites! There's something about salt water that is so therapeutic. Plus, it's free! If you can't make it to the ocean, or it's not swimming season, having a salt bath is just as beneficial.

### 25. Love yourself

It's actually the quickest and easiest way to lighten your energetic load on the planet. In fact, if you master this one, you won't have to make an effort to do the rest of the suggestions on this list. When you love yourself, you automatically want the best for you—physically, spiritually and mentally—and you take whatever action you need to look after yourself. You don't have to be coerced or force yourself to do these things; it comes naturally.

If you'd like more suggestions on simple, practical ways you can uplift yourself, there are more examples my first book *The Power of You: How to positively influence people, places and the world*. You can order your copy at www.drmahdimason.com.

As you can see, there are so many different things we can do to reduce our impact on the planet both physically and metaphysically. I'm sure you could think of many more too. Knowing this, every single one of us can start helping the planet more effectively right now.

# Chapter 7: Physically healing the Earth

After you've connected with Mother Earth and embraced your feminine energy, the real Earth healing can begin—the giving back to Her. As discussed previously, you can reduce your physical and metaphysical footprint and you can give back physically and metaphysically. This chapter focuses on the physical action you can take to contribute to the Earth's wellbeing.

One of the most beneficial things you can do for Mother Earth is to recreate healthy, abundant ecosystems. The more similar they are to what naturally occurred there prior to human interference, the better. Whatever was initially there should be able to sustain itself.

Any life you can give to an area that has none after human interference is beneficial. However, you will establish an area that requires little maintenance if you aim to create an environment that is similar in species composition to the original one. The soil will be suitable for the plants to grow, the rainfall will be enough for all the living things to survive on and the animals will have the right materials from which to make their homes with.

This is all assuming that the area hasn't been so contaminated, re-contoured or drained of nutrients by human activity, that it is nothing like the original foundations of the pre-existing ecosystem. If an area has been badly destroyed, remediation works will be needed prior to attempting to rebuild a healthy environment. You may need to engage an environmental specialist to help you.

Reinstating ecosystems doesn't have to be on a large scale either. If you have a large property and the space to restore large areas, that is fantastic, but it's not the only option for people wanting to give back to nature. You can create a small healthy space in your backyard, if that's what is available to you. Any area that you can help to restore is better than none at all.

## Recreating healthy ecosystems

A healthy ecosystem supports life at all levels of the food chain—from plants to herbivores, carnivores to omnivores, scavengers and decomposers. Having a diverse range of species (greater biodiversity) and an abundance of individual lower order critters (such as insects) is a good sign that the ecosystem is in good health.

Monitoring lower order animals (such as insects) as a means of measuring the health of an ecosystem is also much easier than monitoring larger animals. This is because bugs are much easier to find. They are always in larger numbers so your chances of seeing them are greater, unlike larger animals—which you could spend days looking for before spotting one (the fact that most animals like to hide from people doesn't help).

If you're interested in building a healthy ecosystem, but are stuck with where to start, think of the food chain and start from the ground up. First you need grasses and plants that get their energy from the sun and don't depend on other living things to survive (in general terms). As soon as they are established, the next order in the food chain will have food. Once the next order is established, the next one up can move in and survive. And so on.

You may be reading this and thinking that it is all well and good to want to go out there and rebuild ecosystems, but you don't have the land or the resources to do so. People who live in units, for example, wouldn't have land available. If this is you, don't fret. You can always join a local organisation that is already working hard to restore natural areas in your vicinity.

Organisations such as Landcare and Greening Australia (there are similar organisations all over the world) are always looking for volunteers. The best thing is that they have already done the research into which species need to be planted and have paid for the materials.

Another way of working out what you can do to give back to Mother Earth is to think of all the things she physically gives you and do something to give back to each of those. For example, as she gives us all the food we need to survive, you can give her something to help her grow food. As She gives us all the fresh air we need, we can help her by planting more trees to suck up our carbon and produce more oxygen. As She provides us with clean water from the sky, we can ensure the water we release into catchments is clean and uncontaminated. As She provides us with animals to eat, we can make sure the populations of animals are well looked after. The possibilities are extensive.

## Let it burn

One thing that modern society seems to have forgotten is the importance of fire in rejuvenating the land. Traditional custodians used fire as a major tool in their agriculture. It helped their land to keep producing food and materials for them to use.

Many people often only think of fire as helping Aboriginal peoples as a means of cooking food, providing warmth and protecting them from prey. Little do people realise that fire was also used to sustain the land.

Fire not only creates nutrients for the soil, it has the ability to awaken dormant seed banks buried within it. In fact, many tree species depend on fire as part of their life cycle. Without fire, our lands can become depleted of nutrients and unable to regenerate life.

As so much land on Earth is now private property, the use of fire to keep land healthy has seriously declined. But it is extremely important in sustaining ecosystems, nonetheless.

I'm not suggesting you go out and start lighting fires wherever you like. You will be arrested. However, fire does need to be put back on the agenda for effective land management. The more people who are aware of the benefits of fire, the more likely it will be re-introduced as common practice.

Essentially, anything that you do to physically help the health of an existing natural environment, or to create a natural environment, is helping Mother Earth. It is giving back and is desperately needed at this stage of our evolution.

## 15 ways to physically give back to the Earth

Below are some suggestions of other things you can do around the house, in the workplace and in the community to help Mother Earth.

### Around the house

**1. Practise permaculture**

Permaculture, meaning permanent agriculture, is the creation of perpetually producing, self-sustaining agricultural ecosystems to grow food and provide for other household needs. Permaculture systems use free, sustainable energy and resources (such as sun, wind, water and biota) wherever possible. These systems are energy efficient and are designed to require little external materials or management.

Once set up, any waste generated from the produce goes back into the system to be utilised by something that can benefit from the waste and break it down. Therefore, nothing is unused, much like a naturally occurring ecosystem.

Bill Mollison—an Australian who spent much of his life learning from the natural environment and Indigenous Australians on how to live in harmony with the land—is considered to be the father of permaculture. He, along with David Holmgren, published numerous books on the subject and essentially suggests that agricultural systems should work with nature, rather than against it. They also point out that such systems can provide much more than food, whether it be shelter or replacements for everyday consumables. All with minimum labour and without depleting the land.

An example of a simple permaculture system is a garden that produces food; the food is eaten by people, their bodies turn the food into human waste, the waste is sent to a compost toilet, the microbes in the toilet break down the waste and create nutrient rich fertiliser that can be placed back into the garden to help vegetables and plants grow. And so the cycle continues.

By establishing a permaculture system, you basically start to include yourself in the natural energy cycles of your environment, rather than excluding yourself or being separate to them (which is the way most people are living these days and, as previously discussed, is a major problem in the way we are treating the environment). You once again become an active, contributing component in the cycles, instead of someone who only takes from it. You give back to nature.

Setting up permaculture systems can be challenging. They require detailed knowledge on the subject and can be time consuming and costly to get started. In addition, large systems require land and space; something that not everyone has available. Once set up, however, these systems require much less attention.

It's also important to remember that it is okay to start small. Every little bit helps and is a step in the right direction. Just introducing one little component still benefits the environment and, over time, you can add to it. Even if you lived in a unit, you can develop a small-scale system: grow your own potted vegetables, put your food waste in a worm farm and then use the worm castings back in your pots.

To learn more about where to start, you can find loads of information on the internet and at the library. In addition, most cities will have somewhere that runs courses on permaculture; whether they are short, introductory workshops at community gardens, or more in-depth courses at tertiary institutions. Many local community gardens and community groups also welcome volunteers that have a keen interest in permaculture. You could offer your time and services, while learning at the same time. Check the internet to find your nearest facility.

I have placed permaculture as the number one thing you can do around the house to physically give back to Mother Earth, because I see it as the ultimate way to be kind to the planet within the bounds of your property. It enables you to give back to Mother Earth with nearly every single household activity.

Once you see how efficient nature is at breaking things

down, transferring energy and supplying goods for you, you will likely become addicted to permaculture. (Warning: You may also lose friends because it will become the only thing you ever talk about; don't say I didn't warn you!)

2. **Start composting**

    If setting up a permaculture system sounds a bit too daunting right now, you can ease your way into it by starting to compost your organic waste. Composting not only reduces the amount of waste you are sending to landfill, it also provides nutrients for the soil that can then be used by other plants and animals to help them grow.

    Composting is very easy to do and you can put much of your food waste in there. Have a look online for specific instructions on how to start from scratch. In the interest of the environment, it would be best if you could upcycle something you already have to become a compost bin. If that's not possible for whatever reason, you could search for a second-hand one. Failing that, gardening and hardware stores sell compost bins.

3. **Plant native, local plants and trees**

    Not only will they need minimum maintenance, they will provide food and shelter for native wildlife in the area also. Plants that attract native bees are needed due to the worldwide bee population crisis. So, if you are looking for somewhere to start, a bee tree could be it. (You could even buy a hive of native stingless bees to inhabit and pollinate your garden.)

4. **Utilise your grey water**

   Just because *you* can't drink it, doesn't mean your yard can't. Grey water is the relatively clean water from your bath and shower, bathroom sink, laundry and kitchen. Basically everything except toilet water. It is not to be confused with black water (yep, poo water).

   Untreated grey water can be used for things like the toilet, laundry and general irrigation of the garden and yard. However, if you'd like to use it for watering food plants, it should be treated first.

   Grey water is great to re-use because it not only provides the land with the sustenance of life (water), it also contains some nutrients that your garden can benefit from. In addition, it prevents the need for as much fresh water to be used by your household.

   There are grey water diversion systems and grey water treatment systems. If you, like me, aren't super handy around the house as I am, it's best to ask a professional to come and install one for you.

5. **Give a gift to the Earth**

   It could be a crystal, some food, or an offering of some sort. In Andean tradition, there is a belief that Mother Earth likes sweet treats such as chocolate. It doesn't really matter what it is, if you offer the Earth a gift with the intention of saying thank you for all that She does for you, She will greatly appreciate it.

**In the workplace**

1. **Add more greenery**

   Both indoors and outdoors (if you have the luxury of space outdoors). The more plants, the more you are helping Mother Nature to support you. Plants take our exhaled carbon and some denser metaphysical energy, and provide us with oxygen and higher vibrational energy. You could have pot plants, a vertical garden, or even a vegie patch (mobile versions can easily go inside, as long as they have access to sunlight).

   If your work place occupies outdoor land, planting trees wherever you can will be very advantageous for the environment.

2. **Organise a team building day at a local land restoration project**

   Rather than sending your staff to a typical corporate love-in to build team relationships, send them somewhere they can get fresh air, improve their health, work together and help nature.

3. **Collect money for organisations who are giving back to nature**

   If you can't manage to persuade your colleagues to do either of the above, perhaps you can get them to cough up a small amount of money to support organisations that are doing great work to give back to Mother Nature. If they won't open their wallets out of the kindness of their hearts, perhaps run a raffle or a morning tea to raise money.

4. **Support your environmental staff (if you have any) and their initiatives**

    Often environmental professionals find it hard to compete against their profit hungry counterparts to get environmental projects over the line. The support of any co-workers is always much appreciated, speaking from experience.

    If your organisation doesn't have an existing environmental officer, you can always volunteer to become the representative. That way, you can implement environmentally friendly practices and ensure your employers are giving back to the Earth.

5. **Give native seedlings as gifts**

    Rather than a bottle of wine or chocolate, give something that will physically help the environment once planted. Plants are also a great gift idea for special guests. You could even include interesting facts about that particular species to help the receiver appreciate it more.

    Many people you work with will have children; planting and nurturing seedlings or a tree could be a fun family activity.

**In your community**

1. **Become familiar with existing local environmental projects**

   The more you know, the more you can get involved. Your local council should have information on anything happening in your area. Alternatively, you can search the internet.

2. **Vote for people who take the environment seriously**

   The people you vote for are the ones who are going to introduce policy and legislation. What they implement has a large impact on the places they govern. Therefore, if those people are more interested in development and economic growth than protecting the environment, they will allow significant damage to occur to nature in your region.

3. **Report public areas and government-owned areas that need restoration**

   You might notice a creek wall that is badly eroded and taking down trees, waste that has been illegally dumped, or a place that is visibly unhealthy and needs help. Let the responsible government body (local, state or federal; if you are unsure, ask your local council) know so that they can take action.

4. **Apply for funding**

   Have a great idea to help the environment, but no funds?

Many governments offer funding for such projects. You need to be proactive—apply for funding and explain how your idea will benefit nature and the community.

5. **Engage schools**

    Don't be afraid to let your local schools know when you have a project that you think would be fantastic for kids and teenagers to get involved in. The more young people that are learning about the issues facing the environment—and what they can do to help—the healthier our future will be.

These suggestions are just to give you an idea of the sorts of things you can do to physically give back to the Earth. There are thousands of other things you could do. Once you establish a strong connection with nature, you will think of plenty more ideas. Better still, you can ask Mother Earth what she needs and then listen to what she says. Have fun and be creative!

# Chapter 8: Metaphysically healing the Earth

Have you ever taken the time to intentionally send energy to something or someone? In essence, that's what metaphysical Earth healing is. It's sending energy that most of us can't see into the Earth in order to re-energise Mother Earth. It is very much required for the health of the planet.

Doing such a thing was never considered a crazy idea for our Indigenous ancestors. It was a way of life. They understood that the Universe is made up of all types of different energy—some more dense and solid (what we can see) and some not visible to the naked eye (or should I say untrained eye?).

Our ancestors understood that they received these different forms of energy from their environment, whether through physically ingesting them (i.e. through eating, drinking and breathing), or through their metaphysical energetic systems. They also knew how the natural energy cycles worked on the planet. If they received energy, they needed to give some back in order to keep the energy flowing. Only then could the natural world continue to support them.

These peoples had respect for all the different life forms and energies around them. They didn't assume that they had rights to everything. They didn't take from the environment without first asking the spirit of what they were planning on using; and they thought about the impact of their actions on the rest of the natural world.

Energy is energy, whether you can see it or not. You can't see Wi-Fi, but you can't deny it's real. The same goes for magnetic forces and X-rays. We live in a world filled with non-visible energies swirling around us at every given moment. Why are so many of us so naïve as to believe that we are not impacted by those same energies that affect Mother Earth?

We all have the power to direct energy with our minds with our intentions. It's time we all start awakening to the power of our minds and use them to create a healthier world. It's time we all start living more consciously.

It's not an impossible feat. Our ancestors have already shown us it's possible. All we need to do is start listening to our inner guidance—like we did as children before the outside world told us we were silly. We already have all the knowledge and wisdom inside of us; we just need to tap back into it.

The greatest thing about giving back to the Earth metaphysically, is that it is incredibly simple, absolutely free and instantaneous. Once you understand what you can do, you'll be giving back at any spare chance you get. You'll probably also start wondering why you haven't been doing it your whole life.

*There are two main ways you (and everybody else) can start giving back metaphysically RIGHT NOW. One is to begin giving thanks for all the things Mother Earth provides for your survival. The other is to send love into her.*

## Healing with love, gratitude and intention

You can give gratitude for food, water, shelter, fresh air, beauty and the other incredible things she gives us. It is simple. All you have to do is give heart-felt thanks to the Earth for all that it does for us, regularly. You don't even have to say it aloud.

To get in the habit, try giving thanks before each meal. Sitting down to eat acts as a good prompt. Give thanks for the nourishment that the natural food provides you and all the energy Mother Earth has gone into creating it for you.

Another simple way to give back is to appreciate all the incredible things in nature. It could be particular animals, landscapes, beaches to swim at, or places to hike. When we take the time to acknowledge it, we notice how stunning and enjoyable the natural world around us is even more. Being in nature does wonders for our health and level of life satisfaction—surely that deserves heartfelt recognition?

Sending love into the Earth is also incredibly easy. You can either simply say 'I send love into the Earth' and allow it to happen for a minute (or as long as you like really), or you can visualise it. Imagine a channel of white light, or love, flowing from your heart, straight into the Earth.

How do you know it's working? I can guarantee that if you set the intention, you will have been succeeded, and the Earth will have benefited. Universal law is that if you set the intention, you create action.

But if you are one of those people who need more validation, feel into your heart. Does it *feel* like it's working?

The stronger the feeling, the more energy you are sending. The more energy you are sending, the more powerful you are healing (yourself and the Earth!).

For those looking for more intensive methods of giving back, you could conduct a sacred ceremony with the specific intention of sending love back into the Earth. I understand the term 'ceremony' may be a bit foreign for some people, but ceremonies are really about beauty paired with the power of intention.

Ceremonies allow you to increase the amount of energy you put into whatever your focus is. A ceremony can be done in solitude or with other people who have the same intentions. They can be held in silence, be small affairs, or loud public events with hundreds of people, music and dancing.

You probably wouldn't hold a ceremony every day, given the time and energy required (and how little of that we tend to have due to our modern, busy lives). For most of us, once or twice a month is more likely doable. Holding ceremony on the new and/or full moon is a great way to remember, as we tend to have some idea of what the moon is doing.

They also don't have to be long, drawn out affairs either. Remember, it all helps. Work within your means and give the time and resources you can afford. Also pay attention to what feels right. Sometimes ceremonies might last a couple of hours, sometimes 15 minutes.

## 5 ways to increase your intention

The more intention you place behind your actions, the more energy you send into the Earth. How can you increase your intention, you might ask? You add more energy to your actions.

1. **Song and dance**

    Well-demonstrated by the Aboriginal Australians who understand that movement, singing and sound—when done with intention—puts more force behind what they are trying to achieve. If they wanted to change the weather, they would put lots of energy behind it through song and dance. The increased energy would help them to go further in their feats.

2. **Music**

    Music is sound energy. The louder, more upbeat and more instruments used, the more power it has. Set an intention to the music and it will drive that aim much harder than without it.

3. **Celebration**

    When you hold a celebration in honour of something, you invite other people in to put their power behind the intention. The more people, the more influence you can have. Celebrations often involve music and dance also, so a celebration can be an extremely powerful way of increasing the effectiveness of your efforts to achieve something.

4. **Ritual**

    Creating a ritual to give back to Mother Earth requires intention, physical, spiritual and mental effort. All add to the positive impact you can have in giving back to her. There are no rules to creating a ritual. You can do whatever you feel is suitable. The main thing is that you carry out your ritual with purpose.

5. **Fire**

    Creating a small, controlled and contained (sorry pyromaniacs!) fire with the intention of helping the Earth gives back metaphysically as it helps Her to remove the energies that slow down and restrict the natural energy flows of the environment. Fire clears spaces of old, stale energy to allow fresh, lighter, higher vibrational energy to take its place. Even lighting a candle with the intention of clearing dense energy is beneficial.

## 5 ways to energetically give back to the Earth

There are many different things you can do to help the Earth metaphysically. Below are some further suggestions. The key to all is setting your intention first.

1. **Educate**

    By far, one of the biggest non-physical gifts you can give to the Earth is to teach others how to care for Her both physically and metaphysically. Start by educating yourself on the things you can do to help nature. Even if you only pass on this (incredibly wise and witty) information in this book, it will go a long way towards restoring the health of the planet.

Education is important for all generations—though teaching children in particular will have an impact that lasts long into the future. It will help the Earth (and all living beings) for years to come.

You can educate through social media, by putting information up on community boards, sharing information with your friends and family in conversations, talking about environmental issues in your workplace or by becoming an ambassador for an environmental organisation; just to name a few.

Remember, leading by example is a fantastic way to educate others also. Don't be afraid to show people that you are re-using items, rather than throwing them away, or picking up rubbish in your local area. The more people see others doing such things, the more inclined they will be to follow suit.

2. **Give to Mother Earth anything that is no longer serving you energetically**

This is usually in the form of emotions (which are just a form of energy in our energy field). How many of us carry around old emotional wounds? They do nothing beneficial for us. All they do is keep us stuck in the past, feeling oversensitive and operating at a lower vibration.

Mother Earth knows how to deal with our emotions. We are all her children, after all.

She wants us to be happy. All we need to do is ask her to take them from us. She is ready and waiting.

Go and find a space in nature (or at least on a patch of grass), sit or lay down and ask Mother Earth to take whatever emotional wounds are troubling you. Then allow her to pour her rejuvenating energy into the voids where those emotional wounds once were. It will leave you feeling amazing and it helps the Earth at the same time.

Another trick I use is to stomp whatever it is that is bugging me into the Earth. The things that I just can't seem to shake. Stomping helps to loosen and release them, and drives them straight into the Earth. Realising this method works for me made me wonder how much wisdom we innately have as children that we turn a blind eye to over time. As you will know, kids love foot stomping when they are mad. They know that doing so will literally relieve them of their dis-ease.

Along the same lines as stomping; moving, shaking or dancing your whole body can also help to release stagnant energy. It increases the energy flow in your body and puts more force behind removing any physical and energetic blockages.

3. **Love yourself, look after You and have fun**

Loving and looking after You, in addition to enjoying life, are ways of gifting the environment. As you are not separate from the Earth, anything kind that you do for yourself, you do for Mother Earth also. This also includes believing in yourself and going after your dreams. These are the things we were always supposed to do in our lives, but that we forgot due to societal pressures. When we remember to do them, we make Mother Earth proud and happy—they help her to be healthy too.

4. **Honour spirit**

    Acknowledging spirit—the forms of consciousness that cannot be seen, but which flow through the entire Earth and all living creatures—helps it to do its job of bringing life and wisdom to the planet. Acknowledging that it exists enables us to hear its guidance, in addition to helping it expand and flow.

    When we don't believe in spirit (many people don't in our current day and age), we reduce its power and therefore its ability to help and support all that live on the planet. We also restrict the movement of spirit. It's like we put up barriers that prevent spirit from reaching all the places it needs to go in order to keep the environment and us healthy.

    If you visit a place in nature that is not healthy, you can be sure that Indigenous peoples would advise you that the spirit of the place is unwell also. To bring it back to health, they may dance and sing to call spirit back in.

These people understand the importance of having spirit around to look after Mother Earth and us.

When we honour spirit, we give our thanks and support to it. It opens up our channels in our bodies for energy to flow freely again. That means more energy returning back into the Earth after it's done its work inside of us.

## 5. Welcome the wisdom of traditional land stewards and ancestors

Wherever you live, you can be assured there have been generations upon generations of first peoples who once took care of the land. Their wisdom is unsurpassed. You can ask for their help to look after your land by talking to current generations, or by calling on past generations in spirit.

Many towns will have cultural centres designed to share the wisdom and culture of the traditional land stewards with anyone who is interested. This would be a good first port of call for anyone interested in learning more about to look after the local land sustainably. In Australia, there is also an organisation called Wayapa Wuurrk, which runs courses on getting connected with the land and taking care of it based on Aboriginal tradition.

In regards to asking ancestral generations for their help, all you need to do is ask their spirit. Although they have passed, they still care for the land and they are willing to help when asked. If this is new to you, all you have to say is, 'I ask forward the traditional custodians of the land to help me to look after it'. Even if you don't sense anything after you do it, be sure that your request has been heard and they have been invoked.

Seeing how modern civilisation has decimated much of the lands on Earth is disturbing for those who took so much pride in looking after it. They will take any chance they can get to come forward and help Mother Earth once again. And they will thank you for it.

Simply acknowledging the traditional custodians of the land wherever you travel gives them more freedom to exist and continue to look after the land. It is well worth doing.

Mother Earth depends on the return of both physical and metaphysical energy. By ensuring we give her back these things after we have utilised them for ourselves, we keep her happy and functioning optimally. That also means we keep us (and all living things) happy and functioning at our best.

# Chapter 9: The end game

The little things we do every single day really do help the state of the planet. Little by little, we change our lifestyles to be better custodians of the Earth. But it's good to have something to aim for—an end point that we can work towards.

Having a goal leads to the manifestation of that goal. It's the first step in creation. Think of it like making a wish and sending it out into the Universe.

There's a term used by the Four Winds Society—'Dream the world into being'. In other words, focus on what you want to happen so that the Universe can make it happen for you. In terms of Earth healing, it's imperative we keep dreaming a better world into being.

This phrase is not too dissimilar to the phrase, 'Your thoughts create your reality'. Because you have the power to change your thoughts, you have the power to change your reality. When it comes to being kinder to the environment, we need to ensure we are thinking about the world we want to create, not all the problems that currently exist.

Focusing on the problems will only make them bigger. What you give attention to grows. Worrying about what will prevent us from achieving what we want will only slow down our progress. We need to keep our eyes on the prize.

In fact, worrying about anything limits our potential. It lowers our vibration and keeps us operating in a smaller circle of consciousness. Worrying literally restricts our ability to rise above problems, see things from a higher perspective and find solutions to problems.

When we dream about the changes we want to see, we are in a higher state of consciousness. The thoughts are light and can travel further. As such, they have a further reach of potential and cast a wider net to catch solutions to problems.

Dreaming means we think about what we want, not force it. We dream and then we let it go. We trust that it is all that is needed for the Universe to create what it is we have asked for. Trying to control how or when will only restrict the energetic flow of manifestation and either slow it down or prevent it from happening at all.

We are the leaders in changing the way humans treat the planet. Therefore, we need to take control of our thoughts and make sure they are creating the world we want. We need to understand our own power when it comes to our ability to manifest.

## 10 ways you can manifest healing for Mother Earth

In terms of Earth healing, there are some general things we can all focus on to help make manifest for Mother Earth. Of course, you can add your own ideas, or not use the following at all. The following simply acts as a guide in case you are wondering what you could dream about.

1. **Dream that all people are completely connected to the Earth once again**

Just like our Indigenous ancestors were. This means that the entire population understands that we are part of a larger system in our environment. What we do affects the system and vice versa. How we treat ourselves is how we treat the Earth. How we treat the Earth affects us.

Dream of a world where everyone is so connected to the Earth—that they can listen to it and know its need to be healthy. More than that, dream of a world where people know when and how to act to help Mother Earth when she needs it.

2. **Imagine everybody doing their bit to keep the natural energy cycles of the planet flowing**

That means imagining every single person in the world giving energy back to the Earth. That when people take, in whatever form—food, water, life force energy, etc.—they give back to it in some way, shape or form. They complete the cycle of energy to keep it flowing and the Earth in a perpetual state of creation, transformation and decomposition. Doing so ensures the planet is able to continually regenerate and sustain all other life forms.

*Ultimately, we should be aiming to give the Earth back as much energy as we take from it.*

As discussed in Chapter 7, a great way of returning physical energy back into natural cycles after we have used it is to adopt permaculture methods where possible. Therefore, we could picture everyone practicing permaculture in his or her day-to-day lives as a way of keeping the natural energy cycles flowing.

3. **Dream of the efficient use of land and materials**

   That means no wastage! No wastage of energy, space or materials.

   Material items should be used for their initial purpose until they can no longer be employed for that purpose. Then they should be repaired, recycled or upcycled. Sending them to landfill should be the last option.

   Houses should be built in harmony with the land as much as possible. Naturally occurring heat, wind and water should be utilised, rather than importing these. Houses should also only be as large as needed to be to be functional.

   Land, if used for food production, should be used for the most efficient type of food that can be grown there (i.e. whatever is grown should be able to survive in the natural conditions without the need of much human support or materials). That food should then be consumed locally.

4. **Imagine people only taking what the land can afford to give**

   The Earth has a limit as to how much it can provide for living creatures and we need to live within this limit. Just as wild populations of any living things are regulated by their food and water availability, so it should be with humans. Anything else is unsustainable.

Technology has enabled us to artificially manufacture food, but to do so requires materials, water and energy from the Earth. All of which are also limited. Anything artificially manufactured is almost certainly not healthy for human consumption anyway. And, as you'll remember, how we treat ourselves is how we treat the Earth. So if we're not eating healthily, we are harming our physical and energetic selves, and the Earth.

5. **Imagine that all people use only renewable energy sources**

   Most people are already on this bandwagon, but it's good to keep focusing on creating a world where renewable energy sources are the only energy sources used (instead of non-renewable fossil fuels).

6. **Dream that everyone appreciates what Mother Earth does for us**

   I can't wait for the day when the wider population recognises how much Mother Earth does for them (i.e. EVERYTHING!) and appreciates her for it. The sooner this happens, the sooner everyone will want to protect her. So let's start dreaming this into reality!

7. **Dream of a collective respect for all living things**

   Have I mentioned in this book enough times that I'm an animal lover? Just in case you missed it, here it is again—I'm crazy about animals! They all have the right to be here as much as we do. We are not above them; we are equal.

Respecting all living things (including trees and plants, I might add) is an important step in once again living in harmony with nature. All living things play a part in keeping ecosystems healthy and they are all necessary in keeping the Earth healthy.

Dreaming of a world where we once again have respect for everything else around us will ensure we only take what we need and no more. Doing this will keep the environment healthy and able to continue to support us.

## 8. Imagine that there is no more poisoning of our ecosystems

Whether it's household chemicals, industrial waste or other by-products from living, our future world can't have it. The environment is not ours to poison and doing so eventually makes us sick as well. Poisoning the environment poisons us (along with all other living creatures).

## 9. Dream that all humans are balanced

Dream that each person has masculine and feminine energy in equal measure. No more favouring the masculine. Embracing our feminine is imperative for cultivating a sustainable world. It's what we need to be able to nurture our planet, love each other more and look after ourselves as a community.

Thinking about what we want to see in the world is the best way of creating a better future for ourselves, our children and all generations to come. It is just as important as reducing our current environmental footprint and practicing Earth healing. There's nothing stopping any of us from starting to create the world we want right now.

**10. Imagine the end to the belief that physical things will make us happy**

This one's going to require some hard dreaming! It's certainly doable though. Putting an end to the belief that material things will make us happy will prevent the need for so much of the Earth's materials and the creation of so much waste. Not only that, it will help to make people feel more fulfilled in their lives and therefore happier. As Mother Earth loves seeing us happy, it will be an added bonus for her.

# Chapter 10: She will thank you

If I haven't made a strong enough argument about why we should all be giving back to Mother Earth, this chapter should seal the deal. The reason being, when we give back to Her, She thanks us. I've seen it with my own eyes and ears, and I bet you have too!

Besides the physical and metaphysical benefits She provides us daily to sustain our lives, Mother Earth will also go out of her way to show us appreciation when we help her. It is well within her means—just look what a powerful source She is when it comes to storms and volcanos!

## Mother Nature and her gifting ways

There are many ways Mother Nature can say thank you. Sometimes, it may take you a few minutes to process what has happened before your eyes. Don't question it—she wants you to receive her gifts. Stay open to the magic and you will be amazed at what she can show you.

There's no need to feel guilty about receiving the gifts from nature either. It's all part of the energy cycle—when you give, you receive. It keeps things flowing. The more you acknowledge each gift, the more they will keep coming.

## 13 gifts you may receive from nature

1. **Animals showing up**

    This is by far my favourite. Sometimes nature will send

you an animal (or animals) to say thanks for the work you do. Have you ever had an incredible, once-off encounter with an animal that just made you stop and watch in awe? An encounter that only you saw and that you wouldn't have experienced if you happened to be standing there just one minute later?

Perhaps the animal stops and looks at you right in the eye, letting you know that it is very much there for you. When you are in the moment, you know how lucky you are to have just witnessed what you did. You know that it had meaning.

I have had lots of amazing experiences with animals and I am deeply grateful for every single one. I have been on safaris where I see the rarest of species by chance, I have had animals show up while I've been in spiritual initiations (for example, a soaring eagle when I became a Reiki Master) and some that have stopped me in my tracks while I've been hiking.

By far, two of the most incredible experiences I've ever had were with dolphins and dragonflies. The dolphin experience came about one day when I was sitting at the beach contemplating life. I was unsure about my future and I didn't know whether I should carry on trying to do the work I was doing with animals. Then out of nowhere, a pod of dolphins came along and showed themselves right in front of where I was sitting, not 50 metres to the north or south, RIGHT IN FRONT OF ME!

Not only did they show themselves, they did flips and jumps and had a grand old time. The strangest thing was, I had never seen that species before and I had spent a good chunk of my life hanging out at the beach (I've never seen them since). I was ecstatic to see these dolphins and I thanked them for acting as a sign that I should keep going with my work.

The experience with the dragonflies also defied all logic. It was about three years ago in the house I currently live it. I went outside to run some errands and noticed a whole heap of dragonflies just hanging around. Besides acknowledging how beautiful they were and that I was happy to see them, I didn't give it much thought.

Then, when I returned home a few hours later, there were even more of them. A swarm I would say. Just around my house. Not around any of the neighbouring houses. And I didn't have a creek or water for them to be attracted to. It was absolutely incredible! Then, when I woke up the next day, they were gone and nothing like that has ever happened again.

Oh, and then there were the whales that hung around and did tricks my entire wedding weekend. Or the kingfishers that always come and say hello at my regular meditation spot. I really could go on and on about animal encounters!

As I write this, there are two baby Currawongs and their mother outside my window. Watching them uplifts me and reminds me of the wonder of nature. It keeps me motivated and reminds me why I want to do my best to help the natural world.

2. **Abundance**

   Abundance comes in many different forms. It can be money, friendship, love or success. Nature can thank you by helping you with any one of those things. Most commonly though, I see it in gardens.

   It could be an abundance of beautiful flowers blooming, lush and healthy plants, or big juicy fruits. Your garden may grow better than anyone else's in the street, which is funny if you don't even bother doing much maintenance! Things like to grow where they know that there is respect for the Earth.

3. **Love hearts**

   Nature may also thank you by leaving you little love hearts to find around the place. Fallen leaves in the shape of hearts is a common one, but it could also be heart shaped stones or markings on rocks. Clouds in the shape of a heart are another one Mother Earth uses to tell you she loves the work you do for her.

4. **Sound messages**

   Different sounds mean different things to different people. A storm bird's song takes me straight back to my childhood and reminds me to be my authentic self. A cricket reminds me to enjoy the good times of summer.

The wind tells me to stay inside and nurture myself.

Nature can speak to you through sounds. All you have to do is take notice and think about what it means for you. The more you pay attention, the more Mother Earth can guide you and help you to enjoy your life.

I've also been thanked by Mother Earth through hearing specific songs on the radio. It may just be a line that is relevant to a thought you have at that exact moment, or a song that means something to you and is played in a shop or on the radio at the most peculiar moment. You'll know when it happens. It just 'feels' like a message and it will make you feel incredible.

5. **Protection**

The more you are in harmony with nature and do your best to help it, the more it protects you. You may find that mosquitos aren't attracted to you, or that you don't get bitten by bees, spiders or ants that are around you. If you are barefoot, perhaps you will miraculously avoid stepping on any prickles in an area covered in them.

One thing that a lot of people are impacted by here in Australia in the springtime is being swooped by birds. (Yes, overseas friends, in addition to our venomous snakes and spiders, we also have angry birds to contend with. But seriously, it's not that bad here. You just hear all about the bad stuff.) Another way you might notice that nature is protecting you is if you cease to get swooped anymore in Spring.

In general, you'll probably find that all animals and bugs are calmer around you. They don't see you as much of a threat, so they are happier to have you there.

6. **Happiness around you**

As you lighten your load on the planet and start giving in return for all the stuff you take, you will no doubt start to notice that the natural world around you just seems 'happier'. You might notice more birds singing, or butterflies floating around. Maybe these places just seem lighter?

The more you help Mother Earth, the happier she becomes and it shows in your natural surroundings. If living things have a choice of inhabiting a place that feels safe and vibrant, they will choose it over somewhere dense, scary and less appealing.

7. **Good weather**

Have you ever noticed that some people just seem to have all the luck when it comes to weather? No rain on their wedding day, perfect sunshine for their children's outdoor birthday party and nice balmy days for their holidays? Or what about the people who endure severe storms where every other house in their street gets damaged, but theirs doesn't.

They could be being influenced by nature as a way of saying thanks for being an Earth Healer.

8. **Natural gifts**

    Mother Nature loves leaving physical gifts for you to find. Beautiful stones, feathers, shells or leaves are just a few examples of what she might leave for you. You've most likely already experienced this in your life—where you are walking along and suddenly something just stands out. It grabs your attention and you feel like it's just for you.

    Most of the time, these gifts are for you to take home and place around your house as a reminder of how amazing nature is. Sometimes, however, these items are just for you to look at and leave where they are. You should always ask them before removing them from their location. (And don't be shocked when they give you a clear response!)

9. **Dreams**

    Not all of the thankyous from nature are done in the physical realm. Sometimes, you may receive them in your dreams. You could be taken to a stunning, pristine place in nature to simply sit there and enjoy. You could receive an etheric gift such as a crystal from someone or something that shows up in your dream state and hands it to you with love.

    Another way you might get thanks in your dreams is by someone special (such as an Earth Keeper) showing up to tell you how happy they are that you are helping the

Earth. They could even share some of their wisdom to help Her more.

## 10. Synchronicity

As nature is one big synchronistic masterpiece, you could find that it will create some synchronistic events for you also. For example, perfectly ripe fruit may fall from trees, at your feet, just as you happen to walk past. Or an amazing shooting star zooms past right at the moment that you're looking up at the night sky.

Our natural world is amazing and there are so many things to see that will blow your mind. You just have to be in the right place, at the right time. Luckily nature can help with this.

## 11. Rainbows

I don't think anyone can look at a rainbow without thinking that they are pure magic! Rainbows are incredibly beautiful and they make you feel wonderful when you see them. Mother Nature knows this and she isn't shy at showing them to you when have been helping her.

## 12. Gifts from the elementals

Although many people might not see or hear them, the elementals are very much in existence in the natural environment and they are watching how you treat their homes. If you are kind, they can leave you presents.

If you are not, well let's just say they are tricksters and you might find things go missing or other strange events occur. Be sure to know that they will be laughing their little bottoms off at you once you notice something askew. As a fellow practical joker, I must say that have to appreciate some of their efforts.

As for the gifts, you could wake up to find a perfect circle of mushrooms in your yard, or things of beauty left at your front door. If you are super dooper lucky, they may even show themselves to you for a split second. You can develop your relationship with the elements and, over time, they may start to show themselves more and more.

## 13. Love

Mother Earth loves all of us, no matter what. Many of us don't realise this and therefore don't allow ourselves to receive as much of her love as is possible. The second we acknowledge that She is always there for us, pouring us love, the second we feel it and can benefit from it.

Most of us know what its life to feel loved and supported by our physical birth mothers. We have exactly the same love and support from Mother Earth, if only we let that love and support into our lives. The next time you connect with Her, just ask her to show her love for you.

Once you feel this love and support for the first time, you will never feel alone in the world again. You have such a powerful force in Mother Earth behind you, and he is on your side. All you have to do is welcome her.

Besides all the external thanks that nature gives you when you help, one of the best things about giving back to the Earth is the internal thanks you give yourself for doing something good in the world. It feels incredibly fulfilling. There's a part of you inside that knows this is what She has needed for a long time and you feel great for assisting.

As you can see, there are so many benefits on an individual level to Earth heal! On top of Mother Earth providing you with everything you need to be healthy, she also goes out of her way to specially thank you for all the nice things you do for her. What a stand-up lady!

# Chapter 11: We are all Mother Earth's children

If you have ever had an interest in spirituality, you have probably heard the saying, 'we are all equal'. This was explained to me while in meditation once—I was shown a teapot and told that all of us humans are just like teapots. We are all made the same; the only difference is what we decide to fill ourselves up with.

We can fill ourselves with things that will make us happy, healthy and grateful to be alive; it's like filling our teapot with the purest of water. Or we can fill ourselves with negativity, unhappiness and anger; like filling our teapot with thick, oily, black sludge. Either way, one is not better than the other; they are simply choices that have their own consequences.

This is exactly how Mother Earth sees us—as equal. There are no favourites. We are all her children.

## He's not heavy, he's my brother

As people who care so much about the environment and do our best to help it, it can be disturbing when we come across people who don't share the same respect for our planet. They can make us feel angry, disheartened and even physically ill at times.

We see them throwing rubbish out of their car window, killing animals and trees for the sake of it, poisoning their land and wasting insane amounts of goods. We see billionaires, corporations and governments call for the destruction of ancient lands.

Don't let any of it make you hate a fellow man.

Here's the thing, as terrible as those people treat the Earth, they are still Mother Earth's children. She loves them. They can be likened to toddlers throwing a tantrum in a shopping centre—they make their mothers want to tear her hair out (and most likely want to hide from the embarrassment), but their mothers still deeply care for and love them. These toddlers have much to learn. Mother Earth knows this and patiently handles such people. We need to do much the same. Dropping down to their toddler level and trying to fight them there doesn't fix anything. It creates more hate and destruction.

If Mother Earth can love the very people causing her harm, why can't we? We all have a right to be here and experience life. All people. We are all equal.

Don't get me wrong; I am not suggesting you condone the behaviour of the people who hurt the Earth. I am not suggesting you sit back and take no action. All I am saying is that they are living beings and hating them will only take us backwards. Besides, the people doing all the damage are most likely the ones in most need of some love.

We need to start seeing things from a different perspective. In order for modern society to learn how to treat the land right, people have to make mistakes. Just like toddlers who learn to walk by falling over and hurting themselves. These people in society have to do terrible things to understand that those things don't work. They have to learn the hard way. If they don't, they will continue to make the same mistakes for generations to come.

A common term I hear from spirit is, 'everything is exactly how it should be'. As hard as that can be to believe—especially given all the suffering and destruction on this planet—I know it to be true. Everything is in divine order, now and always. No exceptions.

Trust me, I know what it is like to want to fight these people. I have broken down many times at the injustice of how they are allowed to treat the planet. I have cried my eyes out at the sight of a cattle truck driving past with a load of very scared cows on it, and from seeing lands wiped out by bulldozers. I have wanted to punch those people in the face.

I have worked in organisations that have caused major damage to the environment and watched senior executives give no regard to the impacts they have caused. I have fought on the front line in companies, trying to get people to care about how much harm they are causing. I even undertook a three-year study entitled 'Aligning Organisational Environmental Policy and Practice in the Australian Coal Mining Industry'.

*What have I learnt from all this? There's an effective way and an ineffective way to create positive change. Spending your time pointing fingers and hating on others gets you nowhere. It is literally a waste of energy.*

It drains your energy. The energy you could have otherwise spent on giving back to the Earth. The same energy that you could have used creating constructive outcomes, which in turn would have caused less environmental harm. We are all in this together and we need to find solutions to problems rather than fight over who is right (have you tried reasoning with a toddler?).

## Working together for positive outcomes

So how can we take action in a way that's conducive to positive outcomes?

### Voice your truth

The older I get, the more I understanding that speaking my truth is the best thing I can ever do, in any situation. Authenticity is the key to building and maintaining our personal power. Therefore, if you see a need for change in the world, speak up and voice your truth.

If you are unsure what your authentic voice is, listen to your heart. Your truth only ever comes from a place of love. If you want something to change, it needs to be from a place of love. Anything else is change for the ego and that will not lead to good. It could be for a love for the Earth, yourself, others or animals.

Explain to others what you see as needing to change and why. Tell them why it's important to you. Share your wisdom on the topic.

Be sure to take the emotions out of your discussions with these people. Emotions utilise one of the more primitive parts of the brain and relying on them will not foster creative or effective solutions to problems. Demonstrate emotional intelligence and keep discussions at a high level.

One way to do this is to use science and evidence to support your argument, rather than accusations and opinions. Many people will not accept any argument without proof. State the facts about whatever it is that you are trying to protect. For example, if it's an animal, state what it needs to survive, its breeding patterns, population numbers, etc. The more prepared you are when going into discussions like these the more likely people are to sit up and listen.

## Understand their side of the story

Instead of going in on your high horse, telling them why they are wrong and you are right, take the time to understand their side of the story. Walk a mile in their shoes, so to speak. All effective negotiations come from an understanding of each party's position.

What is it that they want to achieve? What is helping them and hindering them from achieving their goals? What good do they do for society? How do they support the local community?

Understanding the other side of the story will help you to build a better relationship. It will create a stronger foundation from which to create change. Best of all, it will show that you are human—just like them—and that you are willing to work together to find effective solutions to the problem.

You have to remember, especially when it comes to business, that most people who work there just want to do their job and go home. They see their actions as part of their job. They do their job so that they can get paid and go home to feed their families.

What they do for a living is not a personal attack on you or the Earth. In many cases, the Earth is not even given a thought. They wouldn't have a clue how much damage they are causing or the ramifications on the ecosystems they are impacting.

When you understand that, you'll realise that often what is needed is education, not war. And you'll be in the perfect position to deliver that education. You'll be in the door, respected and liked by the organisation, rather than an outsider throwing stones. Now that's a powerful Earth Healer!

**Find solutions to their problems, not more problems**

Sometimes, it can be easier to complain and shout obscenities at people causing harm. Let's be honest though, if you can't see a solution to the problem that will benefit both of you, what are you hoping to achieve?

People will often be willing to change their ways if they can see a way forward. If you can provide them with a solution that achieves your goals, while still enabling them to achieve theirs, you will be much more likely to create change.

Make it as easy as possible for the people you are asking to become different. The simpler it is for them to implement the solution, the more likely they will be to do it. Plus, if they are an organisation they will also have the added benefit of having a good news story to tell their stakeholders.

For example, 'We recently altered our operations to help save the endangered golden cockatoo'. See, it makes them look good too!

## Lobby the government

Sometimes people won't want to know you no matter how much you try to do the right thing and involve organisations when trying to protect or help the natural environment. It's an unfortunate fact that many organisations, and people in general, will often not change unless they are required to by law. That being so, sometimes your only option will be to approach the government.

Governments are usually willing to at least listen to people, because people equal votes. Votes win elections. Winning elections gives the government (even the opposition) power. Therefore, it is worth your while to gather all your facts and figures and take your argument to the top.

Signed petitions are a great way to give more power to your argument. Signatures represent people, and, like I said before, people are voters. You can also get interested parties to send letters to your local parliamentary representative so that they know it is an issue for the community, not just you.

The chances of a positive outcome will be much greater if you approach any discussion with government representatives with an understanding of their position and provide them with potential solutions to the problem.

## Believe that change is possible

One of the people I love and respect most in the world is Dr Jane Goodall (chimpanzee expert and environmental champion). One of the things she commonly talks about is the need for change makers to believe that a better world is possible—that we can achieve what we want.

Having an unwavering belief of what can be done if we all put our minds to it gives hope to others. It is essential for inspiring others to take action. All good leaders must embody this trait.

Great change makers must also remain positive over time. No matter what happens, keep your eye on your desired outcome. The second you lose sight of your vision is the second you give away your power.

*We need to stay positive in order to stay strong.*

To not remain positive is to give up. We need to believe that we can create a better future. We need to give others enough hope to try. As an Earth Healer, this is mandatory!

It's also important to remember that you are not alone in this pursuit. Do not fall into victim mentality where you think it's you against the world. Being a victim makes you powerless. What good can powerless people do?

## Help other people

Because we are innately joined to the Earth, helping other people means you are helping the Earth. Helping other people is a form of Earth healing. The list of things you can do to help others is endless, so I'll suggest just a few here.

The suffering of one person (or animal) lowers the vibration of the entire planet, even if by just a tiny bit. That means, the suffering of another affects you and makes your world a denser place to live. That's why I place so much emphasis on looking after yourself as a means of Earth healing; if you don't you'll bring down the world around you.

In this regard, an important thing to remember is that before you help others, you need to check-in with yourself and make sure that you are in a position to help. There is no point offering to help another if you don't have anything to give. Doing so will only make you weaker and then you'll both be in need of help.

In my first book, *The Power of You: How to positively influence people, places and the world*, I talk all about how one of the best things you can do for the world is to be yourself and look after yourself. When giving to others, you need to make sure that it won't negate either of these two things.

> *You are the best tool you have to help others—you lessen your ability to help anyone if you don't honour yourself first.*

One of the best things you can do, which doesn't cost any of your own energy and takes no time at all, is to send people love. Simply visualise sending love (I picture it as a white light but you could picture it as something else) and then them receiving it, all through their bodies. It's so basic but incredibly effective. Your intention is the force behind the energy that drives it to them.

What are some other practical things you can do to help?

Well, no doubt most people think of the material things we can give others when we talk about giving, so let's start with that. It is a good one because anything material has a direct impact on Mother Earth.

Let's be honest with ourselves here, we all have a whole heap of stuff we don't use or need in our houses. There are a lot of people out there who are in desperate need of some of these things to satisfy their basic living needs. Why not let go and do something that can really help others.

Holding onto things won't make you happy, but helping someone in need will. It's so easy to do and your house will feel much lighter and cleaner after you get rid of all the clutter. If you're not sure how to go about giving your stuff away, you could find a charity that will take your things and give them to those in need, or give to your local second-hand store, or use one of the web services discussed in Chapter 6 on which you list items that people can take for free. Once you realise how little you need, you will continue to help the environment through consuming less and producing less waste.

Another way of helping people is to offer to run errands for people who have mobility issues or are unwell. A quick trip to the shops to pick up some eggs or bread would be no skin off your nose, but a major help for someone who can't get around.

Help where you can when people ask for it. Sometimes you will be able to help, sometimes you won't. But be willing to do what you can when you are able to.

If you would really like to do more to help people in the community, but are unsure where to start, there are many organisations that you can volunteer through—Lifeline, St Vinnies, Red Cross, Meals on Wheels just to name a few here in Australia, but there similar organisations exist all around the world.

One of the simplest things you can do to help others is be company for the elderly. But only if they seem to like your company of course! Could you imagine anything worse than being old, immobile and forced to listen to someone you didn't like? It would be terrible!

As the definition of 'helping' someone going through emotional pain is highly subjective, and often driven by self-interest, all I will suggest about helping others in this instance is to be there for them: listen to what they have to say, allow them to feel heard, reserve judgment and believe in them. You don't have to have all the answers and you don't need to rush them to heal. That can only ever be done in their own time.

Help the world by seeing the magnificence in every single person. See the best in them rather than their physical disabilities, addictions, mistakes or wounds. Life is hard for every single one of us and we are all in this together. Trying to always see the best in someone will help him or her to see the best in themselves. What better gift can you give?

In short, to help other people, we must be willing to be kind to each other. Love, forgive and support. It's that easy.

## Helping animals

To me, helping animals starts with having respect for them. All animals have a right to be here, as much as we do. Humans are no better than animals; we are equal.

The more the wider population respects other animals, the less they will be mistreated, taken for granted or brutally killed with blatant disregard. If we all cherished animals, we would do more to not only protect them, but also their habitats and therefore Mother Earth.

Again, sending love is an effective way of helping any animal. The higher vibrational energy uplifts them and puts them more at ease. It's also incredibly easy because animals are so very beautiful!

It's a well-known fact that eating less meat is good for the environment, but it is also good for all of those animals. If you and your family chose to just eat one less meal containing meat a week, you will save animal lives and reduce the number of animals living in horrific conditions. You will make a difference to the supply/demand chain and to our furry friends.

There are many organisations you can financially support to help save both wild and domestic animals. You can also volunteer your time at local shelters, or adopt a pet. You can also temporarily foster animals until they find new homes.

When you purchase an animal, you can rescue one from a shelter or a pound. You will be saving a life. And once you take an animal home, please, with all your heart, treat it with kindness and love. Take the time to understand what they need to be happy and ensure you do the best you can to give them that.

Find out who your local wildlife carer is so that you can notify them of any injured wildlife you see. Better still, if you have the time and resources, become a wildlife carer yourself. It's such a fulfilling and needed role in communities. So many different animals are injured each day due to human interaction—to be able to take care of them when they are in need is a gift in itself.

If you do find an injured animal and do not know who your local carer is, or do not have one in the vicinity, contact your local vet for the best course of action. To ignore an animal in need is to ignore your fellow Earth occupier.

On a daily basis, you can show kindness towards animals by relocating bugs from inside your house to outside instead of killing them. You can find more humane methods of dealing with pests. Or you can learn more about the species that live around your house so that you can understand why they do what they do. You may even come to like some species that you used to hate when you realise how incredible they are.

Another thing you can do to help animals is to stop using them in derogatory terms. 'He's such a pig', or 'She's a cow', are just a couple of examples of things people say without thinking. Phrases such as this degrade animals and the more we hear or say them, the more we see them as beneath us and lessen their value in the world.

Derogatory animal terms are so ingrained in people's

subconscious that they don't even realise how much they internally disrespect many different kinds of animals. The more deeply ingrained the belief, the more okay people are with harming those types of animals, or seeing them harmed.

Changing our language to improve our attitude towards animals may not seem like a big deal, but it is. Language is a powerful creator of social norms and the more peacefully we use it when referring to our furry, shelled, scaled or winged friends, the better off they will be.

Showing kindness towards all other living things on the planet is something we can aim towards as a society. The more we can do it, the better the world will be to live in. You can set the wheels in motion by leading by example. Yes, you.

# Chapter 12: Ascension of the planet

You may have noticed that there is a huge shift in consciousness going on for people around the world in current times. More people are becoming self-aware, ethically responsible and also interested in spirituality (just look at how popular yoga has become in the last 10 years). What you may not have heard is the Earth itself is also rising in vibration—it's ascending.

The Earth is undergoing a major ascension process as we speak. In fact, 2012 was said to be the beginning of this shift—the dawning of the Age of Aquarius. It is said that the Earth has previously been made up of 60% positivity/good energy and 40% negativity/bad energy (in simple terms). However, we are now on a trajectory towards 80% positive and 20% negative.

That sounds pretty awesome to me! Lots more good stuff happening around the world—and lots less bad stuff. We will all be so much happier! People will be kinder to animals, we'll treat the Earth better and we will love more openly. I want in … where do I sign?

What I hadn't really pondered in this whole scenario is what we personally need to do, and endure, to get to that point. There is so much to look forward to. We will get there, but we have work to do in order to get there.

In order to ascend with the planet, every single one of us has to work through our emotional wounds, face our fears and accept our shadow selves—we need to transition. This is no easy feat. It can result in confusion, suffering, the ending of relationships, loss of jobs and incomes, often in quick succession. In short, our worlds are turned upside down.

The transition process is incredibly tough for everyone. It drives some people to the point of contemplating suicide. Having experienced this myself, and witnessing the same for many others, all I can say is, 'Please hold on'. Things will get better, I promise. The world needs beautiful souls like you.

I know how hard it is to go through the process, but I guarantee you it is all worth it. The person that emerges on the other side of transitioning is an unshakable, confident and loving human being who follows their passion and lives the life of their dreams. Everything they want for can be quickly manifested.

Some of you may have heard about the 3D–5D transition (third dimensional reality to five dimensional reality). This is it. We are transitioning from a denser, slower, harder and darker reality to a lighter, faster, more connected and more loving one. And the only way to get there is through the heart. Everything else has to be left at the door.

To get to the new reality, we need to follow our heart, love all aspects of ourselves and be at peace with our past, present and future. We need to forgive all those who have ever hurt us. We need to have love and respect for all—no matter what their choices—and we need to have compassion for all living creatures.

As hard as it may be to accept all the things happening in

your life during the transition, resisting them will only prolong the entire experience. The quicker you accept it, the quicker you can move through it. Be kind to yourself and acknowledge that you are undergoing a huge transformation. For that, you will probably need some space and time.

It's also important to know that you are not alone during this period. Your etheric support network is there to help. All you need to do is ask. Mother Earth herself, your guides, loved ones on the other side, angels, ascended masters, goddesses, deities or whoever you believe in knows what is happening here on Earth and how tough the transition is for each of us.

In addition, there are people here on Earth ready to assist you. These are the people who have already been through the transition. They understand exactly what is happening and what you are going through. Helping people transition is part of their life's purpose. (There are even Facebook groups dedicated to supporting people through the process!)

Perhaps this information is triggering something in you and you are coming to the realisation that you are exactly one of these people. You have already been through the tough times and now you are in a position to help others. If so, please do. So many people are lost and confused at this time and they are in need of all the help they can get.

The whole process will be much harder for those who do not realise what is going on—or for people who do not believe in spirituality, higher order or ascension. To them, all they see is their life falling down around them and for no apparent reason.

These people won't come knocking on your door for help. They may not even accept your help if you offer it. They probably won't have a bar of the 'ascension nonsense!'. In such instances, all you can do is be there for them, hold space and be available if and when they reach out to you.

Be a listening ear and a non-judgemental confidant. Don't force any of your beliefs or healing methods upon the person. Simply allow them to be. Let them see that you are there. Doing so will allow them to feel 'held' by your gentle support—it will do them wonders.

This time on the planet is the time where Earth Healers need to step up. Some people might identify more with the term 'lightworker'. The name is not important. What is important, is that we become the shining lights that lead the way for the rest of humanity.

Trust me, it will be worth it!

## What you can do to help the Earth ascend

We can actually assist Mother Earth in the ascension process. As Earth Healers, that's what we naturally want to do, right? By helping, we can make the process smoother, quicker and less painful for Her and our fellow living creatures. The following lists a few examples of what you can do to help.

1. **Live your life by leading with your heart**

    When you live your life through your heart it ensures that your vibration stays light, that your energetic load on the planet is minimal and that you make decisions in alignment with your highest Self. Your heart always knows the right thing for you to do in any situation. It knows what is in your highest good and the highest good of the Earth. All you need to do is listen and act.

Eventually, we will all be leading with our hearts, all of the time. Until we get to that point, it's important to take the lead and act as role models.

> *Love spreads love—be the person that leads with their heart and inspires others to do the same.*

The greater the number of people that lead with their hearts, the sooner we will get to the point of everyone doing it.

> *Try starting each morning with the affirmation, 'I lead with my heart'.*

Morning affirmations are great for setting your day off on the right foot. They remind you, your subconscious and the Universe what you want to achieve that day. Stating what your intentions are for your day makes it easier for you to come back to them, no matter what comes your way. Affirmations also help you to focus in on what is important so you can let go of all the superfluous stuff.

My morning affirmation is 'I am true to myself, I lead with my heart and I have fun'. Just saying it each day makes me feel good and ready to take on the world.

2. **Stay positive**

It's also very important to keep your chin up and focus on the positives. Especially if other people around you are only seeing negatives. Without people like you who choose to stay strong and focus on good outcomes, we'd have no-one to shine the light for the others. Without the light-bringers we'd all be stuck in a downward spiral with no visible way out.

The more you choose to be negative, the harder it is for everyone to transition. Negativity slows things down and essentially makes everyone feel uninspired, unmotivated and unhappy.

Every little ray of positivity makes the darkness more light, energetically. It makes it more bearable for anyone caught up in it.

*What can you do to foster positivity in your life?*
*How can you bring light to the world, to your home,*
*to your community?*

Have a big-picture mindset and keep your eye on where we are all heading—where we will be once ascension is complete. Know that it will be a brighter place for all. Know that what we are experiencing right now is only temporary. All of this will help you to stay positive.

3. **Don't not get caught up in the hype**

When so many people are going through a hard time, you can be sure they'll want to complain about it to anyone who'll listen. They'll eventually find other people who also want to complain, who will find other people … and it quickly gains momentum. Before you know it, there can be mass hysteria about all the horrible things happening on the planet.

Stay out of it. It's a choice. Worrying never solved anything. What the world needs when all seems dark are people who can reassure others that everything will be fine, in time.

Don't partake in the conversations where everyone is fighting over who is the bigger victim in life. Don't watch the news and don't get worked up when you see people doing crazy things because they're at their wits end.

We need people to remain calm, unaffected, reassured and certain that things will get better. Of course, this is so much easier to do when you have already transitioned yourself! Nonetheless, it's a choice whether or not you let yourself get involved with the negativity of the wider public.

Also be careful not to get caught up in fear. Fear of scarcity. Fear of World War III. Fear that the sky is falling. Fear has a role in helping you to physically survive in life, but it doesn't need to rule every other aspect of it. To be overly fearful will only keep you from living a free and happy life. It will keep you in a life full of self-limiting beliefs and reasons as to why you shouldn't do things—reasons why you shouldn't live life to its fullest. There is no place for fear in the new world, so you'd best get used to feeling the fear and doing whatever it is you want to do anyway.

> *Try an affirmation like, 'I am safe in the world and calm in my heart. I know that all is working out for the greater good'.*

People who don't allow fear to rule them are able to follow their dreams. They believe they can achieve anything they set their mind to. That's the kind of thinking we need to take us into a world where anything is possible; where we have the power to make our dreams a reality.

## 4. Learn how to energetically heal the land

Often if you hear people refer to Earth healing, they will likely be referring to the healing they do to specifically raise the vibration of a place. My definition of Earth healing is slightly more general (i.e. anything that gives energy back to the Earth), however, all of it helps towards making the world a lighter, better place.

Energetic land healings can be for rivers, oceans, buildings, houses, etc. These healings can be for the purposes of clearing away denser energy that is causing the inhabitants trouble, or specifically to help the Earth ascend to the higher reality. I practice this form of healing also.

There are many different land healing methods, however,

the most common ones involve activations of the Earth in specific locations, channelling specific energies into the Earth, placing crystals in the land/water, utilising liquid crystals or energetically re-tuning areas. All are effective means of lifting a space to a new vibration.

The main energetic healings needed during land healings are for water—whether it be groundwater, underground plumbing or surface water, negative ley lines, places that have been subjected to insensitive human destruction or places affected by electrical or microwave energy. All of these can be healed in various ways.

Land healings are also one of the most efficient ways to raise the consciousness of all the Earth's inhabitants. Instead of healing people one-by-one (which is the common practice of energetic healing), when you do a land healing you can heal multiple people (and other living creatures) at once. The healing will be benefit all who reside on the property.

If the people (and other beings) on the property are willing to expand and grow, a land healing will help them to clear out their 'baggage' and start living at a higher vibration. If they are not willing to expand and grow, they will find the new frequency too uncomfortable and will move to somewhere with an energy that aligns with them.

If you would like to learn more hands-on Earth healing techniques, you can enrol in one of my online courses or workshops (visit drmahdimason.com for more information). Additionally, you could search online for other local people who teach land-healing methods.

This is the most exciting time to be on Earth in thousands of years! What is waiting for us will blow our minds with glorious amazement. Now is the time to change for a better world. I'm on board! How about you?

# Author's final word

Given the state of the planet, we can no longer sit back and do nothing. Likewise, we need to do more than just reduce our environmental footprint. We need to take things a step further and start giving back to it. Giving back is not difficult and there is no excuse for not contributing in some way, shape or form.

I urge you, before you put this book down in a few seconds, think about what you will do to give back to Mother Earth.

> *Choose one thing that will be easy for you to do—that you can sustain doing for a long period of time (the rest of your life if possible). Make a commitment to yourself and to the Earth right now. What will it be?*

Before you know it, that one thing will become habit and you will be doing it without having to think about it. When that happens, you will be ready to start giving back in another way, which will become another habit. Eventually, you will be giving back to the Earth in many different ways all the time, with very little effort.

Mother Earth loves you and thanks you, Earth Healer.

## About the Author

Dr Mahdi Mason is an international author, speaker, Earth Healer and environmental consultant. In 2016, she released the influential self-empowerment book, *The Power of You: How to positively influence people, places and the world.*

Her past experience as a sustainability manager, environmental scientist, shamanic practitioner, land healer and yogi, has afforded her in-depth understanding of both corporate environments and alternative healing practices. This has contributed to her unique ability to communicate openly and effectively with people from all walks of life.

With a Bachelor's Degree in Environmental Science (majoring in ecology), a Master's and Doctorate in Business Administration (environmental management), a Graduate Certificate in Animal Assisted Therapy and more than 12 years of environmental management experience, her expertise is further strengthened by her passion for animals and the natural environment.

In addition to spending several years working in remote communities, Mahdi has worked and consulted with several leading organisations, including Anglo American and Disney Cruise Lines. She has also had the honor of being personally mentored by some of the world's leading Hay House authors and shamans.

Mahdi considers herself blessed to have travelled and

worked throughout Australia, the USA, Mexico, Guatemala, Belize, Ecuador, Peru, Chile, Argentina, Switzerland, England, Ireland, Scotland, Spain, Italy, Bahamas, France, Germany, Nepal, Hong Kong, Thailand, Indonesia, Cook Islands, Solomon Islands, New Zealand, Vanuatu, Laos, Uganda, Tanzania, Fiji and Cambodia.

Pursuing her love of nature and challenging herself, she has completed two overnight 100km Oxfam nature walks, summited Mount Kilimanjaro and run the Gold Coast Marathon. Mahdi has also hiked the Annapurna Circuit in Nepal, the Inca Trail in Peru, the El Camino de Santiago in Spain and the Overland Track in Tasmania, Australia.

Mahdi lives in Brisbane, Australia and spends most of her time writing, practicing, and speaking about Earth healing. She invites you to join her global tribe of Earth Healers:

www.drmahdimason.com

Facebook
www.facebook.com/drmahdimason

Instagram
www.instagram.com/dr_mahdimason

Printed in Great Britain
by Amazon